Dining
in the
HISTORIC SOUTH

by Marty Godbey

Illustrations by James Asher

McClanahan
Publishing House

Library of Congress Catalog Card Number: 90 061814
International Standard Book Number: 0-913383-16-3
Cover photograph: The Planters, Marietta, Georgia

Illustrations by James Asher
Front cover photograph by Paul Beswick
Back cover photograph by Frank Godbey
Cover design and book layout by James Asher
Senior Editor, Gloria Stewart

Manufactured in the United States of America by
Arcata Graphics, Kingsport, Tennessee

All book order correspondence should be addressed to:
McClanahan Publishing House, Inc.
P. O. Box 100
Kuttawa, Kentucky 42055
(502) 388-9388
1-800-544-6959
FAX: (502) 388-2717

"Watch an old building with care; guard it as best you may, and at any cost, from any influence of dilapidation. Count its stones as you would jewels of a crown; set watches about it as if at the gates of a besieged city; bind it together with irons when it loosens; stay it with timbers when it declines. Do this tenderly, and reverently, and continually, and many a generation will still be born and pass away beneath its shadow."

John Ruskin

As an aid to travelers, states are arranged alphabetically, with restaurants listed roughly east to west in the "horizontal" states (Kentucky, North Carolina, Tennessee, and Virginia) plus South Carolina, and north to south in the "vertical" states (Louisiana, Mississippi, Alabama, Georgia, and Florida).

INTRODUCTION

Europeans who settled the American South found terrain as exciting as the hope of freedom that brought them here. Mountains, rolling hills, green valleys, coastal plains and swamps—and seemingly endless, generous space—provided abundant game, rich soil and a climate that could range from brisk to sultry, but was seldom harsh.

They colonized the land, defended it from each other and the Native Americans to whom it belonged, and helped to establish a new country. Early settlers from England, France, and Spain were joined by Africans in bondage, Germans and Scots fleeing intolerance, and Irish escaping famine. Together, they developed a unique civilization.

From the beginning, there were hardships: yellow fever, isolation, injustice, over-farmed land, tragic war, and the humility of living in an occupied country. Resistance to change slowed economic growth until recently, but perhaps that very stubbornness forged the Southern character. Any two Southerners, regardless of differences, have more in common than either of them with any Northerner. We understand each other.

And we know how to live; especially, we know how to eat. Our long growing season, lush pasturelands, coastal waters and inland streams keep us fed; adequate space—even in most cities—keeps us polite; and habit keeps us open, generous, and hospitable.

To many, the words "Southern" and "hospitality" are almost inseparable, evoking mental pictures of barbecues under huge trees, lunches on shady porches, and picnics in verdant meadows. We have always shared what we had, even under conditions of poverty; in times of plenty, our tables are laden, and visitors are pressed to indulge themselves.

Utilizing basic Southern foods—corn, pork, greens, poultry, legumes, sweet potatoes, rice, and game—and combining ethnic recipes with learned techniques, Southern cooks created a cuisine unlike any other, with differences within the region. "Low Country," Créole, Cajun, mountain, "Soul" and Spanish flavors are part of our culture, but Southern food grows more diversified all the time.

Innovative methods of preparation give traditional foods sparkle, often in combination with products new to the area. Ready availability of fresh seafoods to all parts of the South has been an important influence, as has an awareness of diet and nutrition.

And some of the South's most exciting food may be found in equally interesting places.

Some taverns that provided food and lodging for early travelers are still in business; other buildings of historic significance have been restored or refurbished and converted into restaurants. Resorts where city-dwellers "took the waters" or avoided summer heat continue to provide stress-free relaxation, and office workers lunch in business structures where their counterparts worked in the past.

Homes, schools and warehouses have been adapted as restaurants, preserving their unique qualities and offering patrons a little history with their food.

Such unlikely structures as train stations, churches, a newspaper building, and a men's club have been successfully converted to restaurants, giving visitors an opportunity to observe at first hand some of the places their ancestors took for granted.

The restaurants included in *Dining in the Historic South* are only a sampling of the many excellent eating places in the South's historic structures; look for others yourself, and you'll find there are no two alike. Because they belong to people who value history enough to utilize old buildings, they are all very special places.

A visit to any of the South's restaurants in historic buildings is well repaid, for an awareness of the past is as easily absorbed as the delicious food, and the diner leaves satisfied in more ways than one.

Using DINING IN THE HISTORIC SOUTH
as a Travel Guide

Dining in the Historic South had its beginnings in file fold-ers, as notes about restaurants in historic buildings were ac-cumulated over a period of years. Gathered from advertise-ments, history books, old travel guides, word-of-mouth reports, and personal experience, these notes grew into computer files, and three of those files became books: *Dining in Historic Ken-tucky*, *Dining in Historic Ohio*, and *Dining in Historic Tennes-see.*

Dining in the Historic South differs from its predecessors in that it covers all ten southeastern states, but the same criteria were used for selection: restaurants were chosen on a basis of historic, architectural, and culinary interest (frequently all three) coupled with business stability, and most are near a major highway.

Many of the restaurants in *Dining in the Historic South* have never received the national recognition they deserve—visitors will often find they are enjoying places patronized chiefly by local residents. The South's tradition of hospitality, carried out in her restaurants, made selection difficult; ulti-mately, choices were made on preservation/restoration grounds. Of the 90 buildings which house the restaurants included, 60 are on the National Register of Historic Places; 10 are National Historic Landmarks. In addition, those chosen all met the final requirement: they are places a first-time visitor would describe enthusiastically to friends.

The author, often with companions, ate anonymously in every restaurant at least once, ensuring the same treatment any hungry traveler might receive. No restaurant paid to be in-cluded or was told of the project until asked to participate. Without exception, restaurant owners and managers have been enthusiastic, gracious, and cooperative, some providing recipes that had never before been disclosed.

As an aid to travelers, states are arranged alphabetically, with restaurants listed roughly east to west in the "horizontal" states (Kentucky, North Carolina, Tennessee, and Virginia) plus South Carolina, and north to south in the "vertical" states. Resource information between text and recipes provides addresses and telephone numbers, and all travelers are encouraged to call before driving long distances.

Laws governing the sale of alcoholic beverages vary greatly. If beverages are available, it will be so indicated in the resource information. Many dry areas permit "brown-bagging," or bringing your own, but it would be wise to inquire ahead.

Symbols used for brevity include charge card references: AE= American Express, CB= Carte Blanche, DC= Diner's Club, DS= Discover Card, MC= Master Card, V= Visa.

Most of these restaurants would fall into the "moderate" category of expensiveness; an effort was made to include all price ranges. Using dinner entrée prices as a gauge, dollar signs are used to indicate reasonable ($), moderate ($$), and more expensive ($$$). Luncheon prices are usually significantly lower, and the amount of money spent in any restaurant is increased by the "extras" ordered, i.e., appetizers, drinks, and side orders.

In traditional Southern service, main dishes are frequently accompanied by vegetable(s), salad, and often dessert, and in these cases, the price is counted as an entrée price.

Few of these restaurants would be considered expensive by East or West Coast standards; if cost is a determining factor, however, most restaurants will gladly provide a price range over the telephone.

Visitors are cautioned that some of the restaurants in *Dining in the Historic South* have a large local following, and their busy seasons may be determined by local events that are often unfamiliar to non-residents. To avoid disappointment, CALL AHEAD FOR RESERVATIONS.

CONTENTS

GEORGIA

KENTUCKY

LOUISIANA

MISSISSIPPI

NORTH CAROLINA

ALABAMA

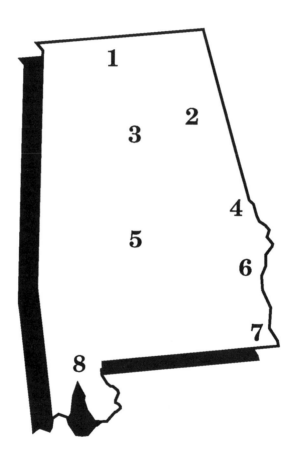

1. DECATUR
   Shelley's Iron Gate
2. ANNISTON
   The Victoria
3. BIRMINGHAM
   Cobb Lane - The Corner Cupboard
   Highlands: A Bar and Grill
4. OPELIKA
   The Greenhouse
5. SELMA
   Major Grumbles
6. EUFAULA
   The Dogwood Inn
7. DOTHAN
   Garland House
8. MOBILE
   The Pillars

SHELLEY'S IRON GATE

Pioneers to northern Alabama rafted down the Tennessee River, battling hostile Indians and rapids at Muscle Shoals, to settle in the fertile green valley at Rhodes Ferry. Despite continued Indian attack and isolation from the Gulf coast, a gracious civilization was established, and in 1826, the town was renamed for Steven Decatur, hero of the War of 1812.

As it grew, the river port became a railroad junction, and although damage was great during the War Between the States, development of adjacent "New Decatur" (later called Albany) in the 1880s revived expansion. The Twin Cities, rivals for decades, merged in 1927, and Decatur prospered as a diversified agricultural and industrial center.

William E. Skeggs, of Huntsville, moved to Decatur in 1871, and was admitted to the bar in 1878. He served in the Legislature and in other public positions, and was appointed Probate Judge in 1896, an office he held for over 20 years. In the early 1900s, he built a Queen Anne-style brick house on Johnston Street in New Decatur, which was adapted to become Shelley's Iron Gate restaurant in 1987.

Betty Shelley opened her first restaurant in 1978, in a shopping center, and named it for its ironwork. "I always wanted an old house," she said, and was delighted to find larger quarters.

The restaurant's cheerful yellow exterior is echoed in delicate pastels in eight inviting dining rooms, including glass-enclosed carport and porch. The homelike atmosphere is ideal for what Betty terms "tea room food", although portions are generous and presentation is never fussy.

Special favorites include Poulet de Normandie (baked chicken and dressing in a cheese-mushroom sauce); Vegetable Lasagna, with three kinds of cheese; and creamy chicken salad— requiring 40 to 80 pounds of chicken breast daily—served with a frozen cranberry-pineapple salad. Soups are homemade, and sandwiches are hearty, and for dessert, there's rich key lime pie and luscious peanut butter pie, although men seem to prefer the homemade banana pudding.

Shelley's Iron Gate, 402 Johnston Street, Decatur, is open for lunch Monday through Saturday, 11 a.m. to 2 p.m. (205)350-6795. Dress is "dressy casual," and reservations are only necessary for groups of 5 or more. AE,MC,V. ($)

SHELLEY'S IRON GATE
STRAWBERRY PRETZEL SALAD

2 cups pretzel sticks
1 1/2 sticks margarine
1 cup sugar
6-ounce package
  strawberry gelatin
One 10-ounce OR
  two 6-ounce packages
  frozen strawberries

9-ounce carton
  frozen topping
8-ounce package
  cream cheese
1 cup sugar

Coarsely crush pretzels into oiled 2-quart baking dish. In saucepan, melt margarine and sugar. Drizzle over pretzels and bake 5 minutes at 350 degrees. Cool. In bowl, mix gelatin and 2 cups boiling water, add strawberries and chill. Blend topping, cream cheese, and sugar; when pretzels are cool, spread with cheese mixture, then gelatin. Refrigerate until firm. Cut through pretzels to serve.

THE VICTORIA
A Country Inn and Restaurant

$\mathbb{A}$fter the War Between the States, vital industries were required to build the New South. Ironmaster Samuel Noble, looking for new ore deposits, purchased land in Alabama; he and Gen. Daniel Tyler formed the Woodstock Iron Company in 1872. A private town named for the general's wife, Annie, was incorporated the next year.

For ten years, the company supported Anniston: paved streets, electric lights, and a water system were built, and the living conditions of workers far surpassed the norm.

When the Georgia Pacific Railroad reached Anniston in 1883, the town was opened to the public, spurring additional growth. Among the newcomers was Col. John M. McKleroy, a prominent lawyer. As President of Anniston City Land Company, a director of the Anniston Pipe Works, the Woodstock Iron Company, and the Anniston and Cincinnati Railway, he built an extravagant Queen Anne-style house in 1888 that reflected his importance.

With its guest and carriage houses, it was placed on the National Register of Historic Places in 1984.

Proprietors Betty and Earlon McWhorter (his contracting

firm did the renovation) and General Manager Dean Robb provide all the amenities of an elegant Victorian home. Towering floral arrangements and comfortable seating greet the arriving guest, and handsomely restored woodwork is brought out by shades of dark green and rose.

Relying heavily on fresh seafood, Robb and Chef Michael Bradford change menus daily, producing innovative soups, homemade breads, and appetizers that are the only recurring items. Specials might be grilled Carolina Swordfish with Lime-Peppercorn Butter, Charbroiled Gulf Shrimp, or Sautéed Utah Rainbow Trout. Pasta, chicken, and pork are always on the menu in some guise, with Certified Black Angus beef, and desserts include varied cheesecakes and an unbelievable Bittersweet Chocolate Terrine.

The Victoria, 1604 Quintard Avenue, Anniston, is open for breakfast 7 days: lunch, Monday through Friday, is 11:30 a.m. to 2 p.m.; dinner, Monday through Thursday is 6 to 9 p.m., weekends to 10 p.m. (205)236-0503. Dress is casual, but most men wear coat and tie, and reservations are requested, imperative during Talladega races in May and August. All legal beverages are served. There are 44 overnight units, including 4 in original buildings. AE,DC,MC,V. ($$$)

THE VICTORIA
BITTERSWEET CHOCOLATE TERRINE

1 cup shelled
  pistachio nuts
1/2 cup golden raisins
1/2 cup candied cherries,
  halved
One 8 1/2-ounce package
  butter cookies, broken
1 cup sugar
1/4 cup water

1 cup cocoa
1 1/2 sticks butter,
  softened
6 ounces semi-sweet
  chocolate, melted
1 1/2 teaspoons
  Grand Marnier
1 whole egg + 3 yolks,
  beaten

Butter 5" x 8" terrine or loaf pan. Peel nuts, soak in boiling water 5 minutes, then rub with towel. Mix nuts with next 3 ingredients. In saucepan over low heat, stir sugar and water until dissolved. Blend cocoa with butter, stir in sugar syrup, chocolate, and liqueur. Add eggs, then fruit mixture, and press into prepared mold. Cover and chill overnight. Unmold onto platter, and slice to serve 10.

COBB LANE RESTAURANT
The Corner Cupboard

The city of Birmingham had its beginning at the intersection of two railroads in Jones Valley, where the Elyton Land Company incorporated a town December 19, 1871, and named it for the English industrial city. Abundant iron ore, coal, and lime brought an influx of workers; the first blast furnace opened in 1880, and the first steel was rolled in 1888.

Rapid growth spurred residential development, and neighborhoods grew into the outlying hills. Many prosperous families moved out 20th Street, and in 1909, the Levert family from New Orleans built a Prairie-Craftsman style apartment house in two sections. As part of the Five Points South Historic District, it was placed on the National Register in 1983.

Left a widow in the 1940's, Virginia Cobb opened a knit shop in the building; she had the basement dug out, creating ceiling height to accommodate the public. Here she established her "Corner Cupboard" tea room, a Birmingham institution for over forty years. French-inspired murals decorated basement walls, and rear galleries overlooked a stone-paved courtyard, creating a "New Orleans" atmosphere.

Even when the neighborhood deteriorated, the restaurant maintained its popularity, and 19th Way was renamed "Cobb Lane" in honor of Mrs. Cobb when new business rejuvenated Five Points South.

Today, Cobb Lane Restaurant is operated by Mary Iris Bond, who carries on the tradition for a third generation of customers, presenting "Southern cuisine with a Continental flair" that includes many of Mrs. Cobb's recipes. Grande dames and secretaries, businessmen and artists still enjoy She-crab Soup, buttery little rolls, and chicken and shrimp salads, now joined by items for the diet conscious. Everyone saves room for dessert, however—especially the light chocolate cake rolled in whipped cream: Cobb Lane's famous Chocolate Roulage.

Cobb Lane Restaurant, #1 Cobb Lane, Birmingham, is between 13th and 14th Avenues, South, off 20th Street. It is open for lunch from 11 a.m., Monday through Saturday. (205)933-0462. Dress is "Dressy casual," reservations are requested, and all legal beverages are served. AE,MC,V. ($)

COBB LANE CHOCOLATE ROULAGE

5 eggs, separated
1 cup sugar, divided
6 ounces dark sweet
  chocolate, melted with
  3 Tablespoons
  cold water

Cocoa
1 cup whipping cream
1 teaspoon vanilla

Beat yolks; add 3/4 cup sugar and beat until thick. Blend cooled chocolate with yolks, then stiffly-beaten whites. Butter a cookie sheet, line with waxed paper, and butter again. Spread mixture evenly, and bake at 325 degrees 10 minutes. Reduce heat, and bake 5 minutes more. Remove from oven and cover with cold wet towel; after 20 minutes, chill 1 hour.

When ready to serve, carefully remove towel and loosen cake from paper. Sift cocoa over cake, then turn cake onto fresh waxed paper. Peel off old paper. Whip cream with remaining sugar and vanilla, spread over cake, and roll lengthwise, as jelly roll. Slice to serve.

HIGHLANDS: A BAR AND GRILL

The rich mineral deposits in the Birmingham area produced steel, coal, and more than 3,000 other products. Industry created residential growth, and "The Magic City" spread into the mountains and valleys. Today, medical and technological institutions are Birmingham's largest employers, maintaining the economy, and the lush green neighborhoods remain among the South's finest.

Near the center of medical activity, rejuvenation of an older neighborhood began when Frank Stitt opened Highlands: A Bar and Grill, in a Spanish Revival commercial building built by the Munger family in the late 1920s. Other restaurants and shops followed, and Five Points South Historic District was placed on the National Register in 1983.

Stitt's food is "fresh and clear and bright-flavored, emphasizing the Southern heritage with the keenest pursuit of the best ingredients." Menus change daily, reflecting freshest Southern produce: corn pancake with lump crab meat; roast venison with sun-dried cherries; mixed salad with pecans, bleu cheese and sherry vinaigrette; or homemade Jack Daniels chocolate ice cream. Whatever is offered the day you go will be great food, beautifully presented, in a comfortable, casual atmosphere. Don't miss it.

Highlands: A Bar and Grill, 2011 11th Avenue, South, is open for lunch Tuesday through Friday, 11 a.m. to 2 p.m., and for dinner Tuesday through Saturday, 6 to 10 p.m., to 10:30 Friday and Saturday. It is closed the last week of August. (205)939-1400. Dress is casual, reservations are suggested for dinner and for lunch parties of 5 or more, and all legal beverages are served. AE,MC,V. ($$)

HIGHLANDS CRAB CAKES

2 pounds fresh
 blue crab meat
3 cups bread crumbs, from
 day-old French bread
6 Tablespoons
 unsalted butter,
 melted and cooled
2 eggs, beaten
2 Tablespoons
 chopped shallots
1 Tablespoon
 chopped green onion
2 Tablespoons chopped
 parsley

2 Tablespoons lemon juice
Pinch freshly
 grated nutmeg
Pinch cayenne pepper
Salt and pepper
2 eggs, beaten with
 2 Tablespoons water
1 cup bread crumbs,
 as above
3 Tablespoons
 CLARIFIED butter
Beurre Blanc*
Lemon wedges

Gently combine first 11 ingredients; adjust seasoning. Form into 8 loose patties, dip into egg mixture, then bread crumbs, and rest on rack. Heat CLARIFIED butter very hot; add crab cakes (two pans may be needed) and cook over medium-high heat until golden, 3 to 4 minutes. Turn and cook until just done. Serve with Buerre Blanc, and garnish with lemon wedges. Serves 8.

*For Beurre Blanc: In saucepan, combine 1 cup white wine, 1/4 cup white wine vinegar, and 2 Tablespoons chopped shallots. Reduce to syrupy glaze. Remove from heat and stir in 1 Tablespoon cream. Reduce, and over low heat, add 1/2 pound room-temperature unsalted butter bit by bit, blending completely each time. Add salt, pepper, and lemon juice to taste. Strain, and keep barely warm until needed.

THE GREENHOUSE

Rich farmlands attracted wealthy Georgians to eastern Alabama in 1836; they named their new settlement with a form of the Creek Indian word for "big swamp." Opelika grew rapidly when the railroad came in the 1840s, and many of the downtown commercial buildings, recently restored, reflect the town's second "boom" in the Postbellum years.

In 1902, Walter Cullars purchased a lot on what was then Tallapoosa Street, and about 1906, he and his wife built a comfortable Queen Anne-style house with a curving porch. When Annie Bell Burkhead bought the property in the 1920s, she enlarged the front room and brought the interior up to date. It remained in her family until 1978, when it was purchased and renovated to become a restaurant.

Owner Ursula Higgins and Chef John Halko present a Continental menu that is nevertheless very much in keeping with the house's gracious, Deep South atmosphere. Ceiling fans, pastel napery, candlelight and flowers create a romantic setting. Despite these welcome distractions, the food demands attention.

Sauces and presentation vary, and the menu changes every two weeks to utilize the freshest products, but always includes chicken, veal, duck, steak, and, frequently, pork. Seafood gumbo and escargot in mushroom caps are popular appetizers, and the more-than-ample chicken salad/fruit plate is a lunchtime winner. Seven or eight varieties of home-made hot muffins alternate, and among the Greenhouse's signature desserts are Pear Frangipane Tart, Rapsodie Torte (flourless chocolate with raspberries) and luscious Lemon Curd Cheesecake.

Lighter fare from a separate menu is available on the recently enclosed porch after 4 p.m.

The Greenhouse, 114 North Ninth Street, Opelika, is on the corner of Second Avenue (US 29), and is open for lunch Monday through Friday, 11 a.m. to 2 p.m., and for dinner Monday through Thursday, 5:30 to 9 p.m., to 10 Friday and Saturday. (205)749-0902. Reservations are accepted, dress is casual, and all legal beverages are served. Busiest times are football and parents' weekends at Auburn. MC,V. ($$)

GREENHOUSE CREAMY TARRAGON DRESSING

1 egg
1 teaspoon tarragon
1 teaspoon dry mustard
1 teaspoon minced garlic
1 teaspoon black pepper
1/2 cup chopped
  green onion
1/2 cup chopped parsley
1 cup tarragon vinegar
Juice of 1/2 lemon
1 cup oil

Place first nine ingredients in blender; blend until incorporated. With machine still on, add oil until there is no more well in the center. Yields about 2 1/2 cups.

MAJOR GRUMBLES

Hernando de Soto visited the high cliff overlooking the Alabama River in 1540, but it was not mapped until 1732. Selma, founded in 1820, grew along the riverbank, and became an industrial center surrounded by great cotton plantations.

A Confederate arsenal, Selma produced cannon, ammunition, and ships during the War Between the States. After the brief but decisive battle in April, 1865, the town was burned and pillaged by drunken Federals, and although its economy gradually recovered, cotton was no longer king.

The Water Avenue Historic District—placed on the National Register in 1972—is the largest Antebellum riverfront warehouse district in the Southeast. Major Grumbles restaurant is in the warehouse next to Lafayette Park, near where the General came ashore on his visit in 1825.

The part of the building enclosed to become a restaurant in 1986 is clean and modern inside, scarcely showing its origin as a cotton warehouse, and later use as a wholesale grocery, but the remainder is still in original condition, and is appropriately used for storage.

Owners Martha and Howard Strickland named Major Grumbles for a colorful local character, and maintain a light-hearted atmosphere in the restaurant, where service and premium products are emphasized, and all foods are homemade.

Hearty sandwiches served on thick homemade bread include thin sliced roast beef, chunky chicken salad, charbroiled ground sirloin, and grilled marinated chicken breast; tasty homemade soups or salads are appropriate to the season, and after 6 p.m., hand cut steaks and special dinners are added to the menu.

For dessert, try to save room for cheesecake with a variety of sauces or melt-in-your-mouth Peach Schnapps ice cream topped with "imbibed" fruit.

Major Grumbles, #1 Grumbles Alley, Selma, is just off Water Avenue at the intersection of Franklin Street, and is open 11 a.m. to 10 p.m., Monday through Saturday. (205)872-2006. Dress is casual, all legal beverages are served, and reservations are accepted, preferred for parties of 6 or more. Busiest times are Pilgrimage (March), Battle of Selma re-enactment (April), and Riverfront Market Day (2nd Saturday in October). AE,CB,MC,V. ($$)

MAJOR GRUMBLES
MARINATED CHICKEN BREAST

4 chicken breasts, boned
1 Tablespoon parsley
1 cup olive oil
1 teaspoon paprika
1/3 cup apple cider vinegar
1 teaspoon white pepper
1 Tablespoon oregano
2 teaspoons salt
1 Tablespoon tarragon
1 teaspoon garlic powder
1 Tablespoon basil

Skin and wash breasts; place in non-reactive container. Mix remaining ingredients in a jar, shaking well. Pour over chicken breasts, cover and seal top. Refrigerate at least 4 hours, 24 hours preferred. Remove breasts from marinade. Grill over hot coals, turning several times, until done. Serves 4.

DOGWOOD INN

Westward migration was in force throughout the country in the early 19th Century; in the South, where soil was depleted by constant cotton farming, successful planters frequently relocated, seeking new land. The Territory of Alabama, created in 1817, drew its new population from nearby regions, and those who settled the rich farmlands west of the Chattahoochee River came primarily from Georgia.

About the time Alabama became a state, in 1819, the town of Irwinton was established on the river. It was renamed "Eufaula" in 1843 for a tribe of Creek Indians. With over 700 buildings on the National Register, Eufaula has a charming mixture of architectural styles: Greek Revival, Italianate, and several types of Victorian.

The Dogwood Inn occupies a 1 1/2 story Queen Anne-style house, whose spreading porch roof is supported by Corinthian columns. It was built as a boarding house about 1905, by a family named Threatte, and, as part of the original Seth Lore Historic District, was placed on the National Register in 1973.

Owner Helen Young offers a friendly, homelike menu that suits the house, with its warm woodwork and high ceilings.

Lunch is not a sideline here; specials might be Baked Chicken with Orange Sauce, or Ham and Artichoke Rolls, baked in a Swiss cheese sauce. Homemade French Onion soup and Gumbo are always available, and others might be Old Fashioned Vegetable Beef, or Shrimp Bisque.

Dinner specials include seafoods, poultry (frequently quail) and hand cut beef—the house specialty Prime Rib is cooked very slowly, resulting in tender, juicy meat.

Among dessert favorites are homemade cheesecakes, pecan pie, and a crêpe filled with ice cream, covered with chocolate sauce, whipped cream, and almonds.

Dogwood Inn, 214 North Eufaula Avenue, Eufaula, is open Monday through Saturday. Lunch is 11 a.m. to 2 p.m., dinner 5 to 9:30 p.m. It is closed between Christmas and January 1, and on Mondays in January and February. (205)687-5629. Dress is casual, all legal beverages are available, and the busiest time is Pilgrimage, usually the first week in April. Reservations are accepted, recommended for parties of 4 or more. AE,CB,DS,MC,V. ($)

DOGWOOD INN HELEN'S PECAN PIE

One 9-inch unbaked
  pie shell
1 cup dark brown sugar
1 cup light corn syrup
1/3 cup melted butter
1/3 teaspoon salt
1 teaspoon vanilla

4 Tablespoons
  Kahlúa liqueur
3 eggs, lightly beaten
1 heaping cup
  chopped pecans
Whipped cream
  for garnish

In large bowl of mixer, combine sugar with next five ingredients. Add eggs and beat for 2 to 3 minutes. Pour into pie shell, sprinkle with pecans and stir in well. Bake at 350 degrees 45 minutes, or until browned—it may still be soft. Cool well before cutting; top with whipped cream.

GARLAND HOUSE

In frontier days, men who struggled with the heavy "wiregrass" in southeastern Alabama had to be as tough as the vegetation, and the town they built was equally rough-and-ready. Its name, taken from the Bible, did nothing to quell its high spirits, but when the railroad came in the 1880s, so did law and order. Industry, based on the abundant longleaf pine, produced lumber and turpentine; when mechanized farming utilized the former pineywoods, Dothan became a trade center, and its prosperous people built fine homes, schools, an opera house, and a hospital.

Near Moody Hospital, a comfortable southern bungalow with a wraparound porch was built by the C.K. Merrill family about 1908. Later, it was a rooming house, then a school, and had deteriorated considerably when Jo Garrett and a partner renovated it to became a restaurant in 1976. A handsome quarter-sawn oak mantel in the front room required a week's stripping, so others were antiqued for the time being, but hardwood floors were exposed, and the high-ceilinged rooms were made bright and cheerful. Antiques and greenery add to the homey feeling, and the food is the kind you wish your grandmother had served.

Jo specializes in crêpes, with Chicken Divan the most popular. There's a crêpe of the day, a quiche of the day, and her own variation of Eggs Benedict. Seafood Gumbo and French Onion Soup are always available, with other cold weather specials replaced by fruit salads in Summer. Sandwiches are hearty and salads are generous, accompanied by crusty little homemade rolls.

Some desserts, such as Hot Mocha Fudge Sundae Crêpe and Bananas Foster Crêpe, are built around Jo's specialty. Just as yummy are chess pie, double chocolate brownie, and a treat developed for Dothan's Peanut Festival (Alabama produces 25 per cent of the nation's peanuts). A crunchy crust is filled with vanilla ice cream, topped with peanut sauce, covered with mocha fudge sauce, and well-named: "Peanut Paradise Pie."

Garland House, 200 North Bell Street, Dothan, is on the corner of Adams Street, and is open 11 a.m. to 2 p.m., Monday through Friday. (205)793-2043. Dress is casual, reservations are requested for parties of 6 or more, and wine is available. Busiest time is during the Peanut Festival in late October. MC,V, personal checks. ($)

GARLAND HOUSE QUICK DINNER ROLLS

1 Tablespoon yeast
2 cups warm water
1/4 cup sugar
1/4 cup shortening

2 eggs
1 Tablespoon salt
4 1/2 cups flour

In mixer bowl, stir yeast into water until dissolved. Add sugar, shortening, and eggs, and mix on low speed until blended. Add salt and flour and beat. Let rise in warm place. Dip spoonfuls of dough into well-greased muffin tins. Let rise, and bake 12 to 15 minutes at 400 degrees.

THE PILLARS

Beautiful Mobile Bay, known to Europeans from the earliest days of exploration, tempted numerous would-be colonists in the 16th century, but it was not settled until the Sieur de Bienville established Fort Louis in 1702.

After a disastrous flood in 1710, the fort was relocated down river at the site which became Mobile. Surviving hurricanes and epidemics, and life under French, British, and Spanish rule, Mobile finally became part of the United States in 1813. An important port on the Gulf of Mexico, the city grew rapidly; handsome houses that reflect its Creole heritage attest to the cultured and prosperous people who built them.

Parker J. Glass, a physician who lived and worked in the downtown area, built a white-columned house on Government Street, at the end of the car line, about 1912. In the Neoclassical style, the house's tile floors, high ceilings, and interior columns, well suited to Mobile's climate, were designed for living on a lavish scale.

By 1926, Guillermo Valenzuela, who had been Guatemalan Consul to Mobile, lived in the house with his wife Adela and several family members. After his death, Adela operated a boarding house there until 1953; it was a guest and tourist home for another 20 years, then stood vacant until it became a restaurant.

Filippo Milone, a Sicilian chef trained in Europe, had made his home in Mobile. With partners, he opened The Pillars in 1976, restoring it to its former grandeur with parts from the identical house next door, and furnishing it with antiques. Immediately popular, the restaurant's intimate atmosphere belies its size—there are 11 dining rooms—and fine Continental food is served in romantic surroundings.

In addition to a menu that includes Certified Black Angus beef, top grade veal, and the freshest Gulf seafood, Milone and Chef Ronald Wilemon offer four nightly fixed-price "Epicurean Dinners." Breads, sauces, and special vegetables are all home-made—don't miss the Spinach Madeline in a jalapeño cream sauce—and popular desserts include Grand Marnier Chocolate Gâteau, Cheesecake Amaretto, and Southern Comfort Bread Pudding.

The Pillars, 1757 Government Street, Mobile, is open Monday through Saturday, 5 to 10 p.m. (205)478-6341. All legal beverages are served, most men wear coat and tie, and reservations are recommended. AE, DC, DS, MC, V, DS. ($$$)

THE PILLARS SALMON WITH SORREL SAUCE

1/2 cup dry white wine	1 cup heavy cream
1/2 cup dry white vermouth	2 ounces fresh sorrel leaves
1/2 cup strong fish stock	Salt and pepper
3 Tablespoons chopped shallots	4 six-ounce filets of salmon

In saucepan, reduce first four ingredients until syrupy. Stir into cream and simmer until thickened. Add sorrel which has been blanched in salted water, drained, and chopped fine. Season the sauce and keep warm. Grill salmon and serve in a pool of sauce. Serves 4.

FLORIDA

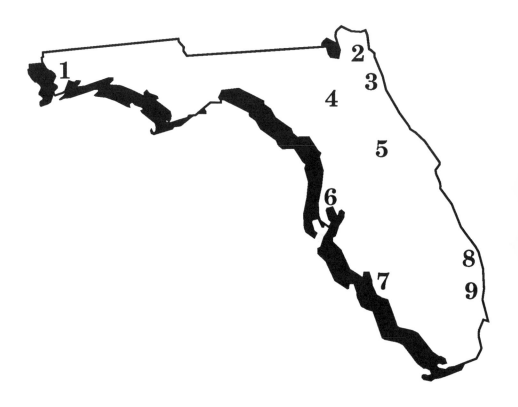

1. PENSACOLA
   Jamie's French Restaurant
2. JACKSONVILLE
   Café on the Square
3. ST. AUGUSTINE
   Scarlett O'Hara's
4. GAINESVILLE
   Toby's Corner
5. MAITLAND
   Jordan's Grove
6. TAMPA
   Columbia Restaurant
7. FORT MYERS
   The Veranda
8. PALM BEACH
   The Breakers
9. LIGHTHOUSE POINT
   Cap's Place Island Restaurant

JAMIE'S FRENCH RESTAURANT

Desirable Pensacola Bay passed back and forth between Spanish and French in the 18th century; after Florida was ceded to Great Britain in 1763, a town was laid out at Seville Square. Recaptured by the Spanish in 1781, the city was taken by Andrew Jackson in 1818, and Florida was transferred to the United States in 1821.

In mid-19th century, harvesting of pine forests in northwest Florida improved the area's economy. Timber was sent by rail to ships at Pensacola, and the city grew beyond the original town, where workers in the shipping industry continued to make their homes.

The Pensacola (Seville Square) Historic District, named a National Historic Landmark in 1970, contains many examples of early Gulf Coast architecture which have been preserved or restored. A vernacular frame cottage now adapted as Jamie's Restaurant existed before 1884; its four main rooms, linked by a central hall and heated by back-to-back fireplaces, are typical, but its starched gingerbread trim and pink clapboards provide a feminine touch—it has frequently been owned by women.

It was a tea room when Chef Elizabeth "Libby" Dasher and

Gary Serafin came on board in 1981 and the cuisine changed to country-style French. Since 1984, they have been owners of a sophisticated restaurant that serves extraordinarily good food in a comfortable, unpretentious atmosphere.

Classic sauces are stressed here: intensely rich and carefully selected to bring out the flavors of fresh duck, lamb, veal, and seafood. Enhanced by crusty French bread, meals provide exciting contrasts—velvety Cream of Carrot Soup, tangy Honey-Mustard House Dressing, savory Scallops in Avocado Beurre Blanc Sauce, and Torte del Rey, a chocolate flourless cake with walnuts and mocha buttercream, that defies description.

Jamie's French Restaurant, 424 East Zaragossa, Pensacola, is open for lunch Tuesday through Saturday, 11:30 a.m. to 2:30 p.m., and for dinner Monday through Saturday, 6 to 10 p.m. (904)434-2911. Dress is casual, but sneakers, jeans, and shorts are not permitted in the evenings. Beer and an extensive wine list are available, and reservations are recommended, especially on weekends and for lunch. AE,MC,V. ($$$)

JAMIE'S SCALLOPS ON LINGUINE WITH RED PEPPER AND CAPER BUTTER SAUCE

1 pound scallops, floured   **1/4 cup heavy cream**
CLARIFIED butter or oil   **Salt and pepper**
1/2 pound linguine,   ***Sauce**
  cooked and drained

In large skillet, sauté scallops in CLARIFIED butter or oil 5 minutes. Keep warm ln 250 degree oven. Heat linguine in cream, season, and keep warm. To serve, place scallops on linguine, spoon sauce over. Serves 4.

*For Sauce: In large skillet, combine 1/2 red pepper, in julienne; 1 clove garlic, minced; 1/4 cup clam juice; 1/4 cup white wine; 1 Tablespoon capers; and 1 Tablespoon chopped parsley. Over high heat, reduce liquid to 1 Tablespoon. Remove from heat and cool slightly; return to low heat, and gradually stir in 1/2 pound butter, bit by bit.

CAFÉ ON THE SQUARE

Andrew Jackson's military successes in the War of 1812 and later Florida Campaign hastened the acquisition of Florida by the United States. When a town was laid out in the double loop of North-flowing St. John's River in 1822, it was named for the popular hero, already suggested as a future President.

Jacksonville's growth, retarded by the Seminole Wars, boomed in the 1880s when it became a luxurious winter resort. Opulent hotels with new electric lights vied for business, and expositions and fairs displayed oranges, alligators, and tropical plants. When tourists moved farther south, the city continued to grow, becoming a busy seaport and prosperous industrial center.

In the 1920s, Florida's land boom affected the whole state; the first commercial building on South Jacksonville's San Marco Square was a two-story stucco Spanish eclectic structure built in 1926. With its suggested central tower and tile roof, it provided an anchor for subsequent buildings on either side.

Purchased by John Currington in 1979, it was renovated in 1984 to become a restaurant. First floor arches removed in a

1930s remodeling were replicated in a new arcade, and interior partitions were taken out to create a spacious dining room with exposed brick walls.

Café on the Square has a relaxed, comfortable feeling, enhanced by Chef Curtis Lowery's American cuisine. Fresh seafoods, poultry, and beef are given interesting treatment— Captiva Poulet de Mer (sautéed chicken breast with shrimp, bacon, and Mozzarella in Dijon cream), Filet Mignon with Sauce Forestiere—and nightly specials of grilled grouper, snapper, tuna or whatever's fresh are served with appropriate sauces. Desserts are yummy and homemade, there's always Prime Rib on weekends, and you'll enjoy the enthusiastic welcome that explains this gathering spot's popularity.

Café on the Square, 1974 San Marco Boulevard, Jacksonville, may be reached by the San Marco exit off southbound I-95, and by Prudential Drive exit, northbound. It is open 7 days a week: Sunday through Thursday 4 to 11 p.m., to 12:00 midnight Friday and Saturday, and for Sunday brunch 11 a.m. to 2 p.m. (904)399-4422. All legal beverages are served, dress is casual, and reservations are accepted only for private parties. AE,CB,DC,MC,V. ($$)

CAFÉ ON THE SQUARE COCONUT SHRIMP

For batter:
1 cup flour
1 egg
1 cup milk
1 Tablespoon oil

Shrimp, deveined and
  shelled, tails on
Unsweetened flaky
  coconut
Oil for deep frying
Dijon-Honey Sauce*

In bowl, mix batter ingredients. Dip shrimp (6 to 8 for appetizer serving, 12 for entrée serving) in batter, then in coconut, turning to coat well. Deep fry in oil at 350 degrees 2 to 2 1/2 minutes, or until just golden brown. Serve with Dijon-Honey Sauce.

*For Dijon-Honey Sauce: Blend 1 cup honey with 1/4 cup Dijon mustard.

SCARLETT O'HARA'S

Spanish attempts to colonize Florida were based on the notion that somewhere in the interior were mountains filled with gold. This rumor, fostered by coastal Indians attempting to rid themselves of the Spanish, only prompted more exploration. After many expeditions to both coasts, the first permanent European settlement was established in 1565 by Pedro Menendez de Aviles.

Fought over for generations, St. Augustine was protected by Castillo de San Marcos after 1672, but was destroyed in 1702, when Spanish defended against invaders from South Carolina.

Many buildings remain from the early 18th Century; the St. Augustine Historic District, named a National Historic Landmark in 1970, contains original buildings and reconstructions that house shops, restaurants, and a living history museum.

On the western boundary of the historic district, a frame cottage was built in 1879 by George Colee and his son William. The Colees, a long-time family of carriage builders, occupied the house until 1924.

In 1979, it was adapted for use as Scarlett O'Hara's restaurant. Although the exterior was changed only by the reconstruction of an earlier porch, interior walls were removed and the second floor opened up; original corner fireplaces remain in what were four ground-floor rooms. Upstairs, downstairs and out on the porch, Scarlett's offers "fun" food, well prepared and simply presented.

Specials might be Smoked Grouper Spread or Alligator Tail, added to made-to-order ground chuck burgers, Chicken-on-a-Stick, a platter of steamed veggies with cheese, and wonderful soups: Tugboat Stew (seafood and beef), French Onion, or a constantly changing Seafood Chowder.

Scarlett O'Hara's, 70 Hypolita Street, St. Augustine, is at the corner of Cordova near public parking. It is open 7 days a week, 11:30 a.m. to 12:30 p.m. (904)824-6535. All legal beverages are served, dress is casual, and reservations are not accepted. AE,DC,MC,V. ($)

SCARLETT O'HARA'S
MINORCAN CLAM CHOWDER

3 ounces salt pork,
  in 1/4" dice
1 cup chopped onion
1/2 cup chopped carrot
1/2 cup chopped celery
Two 28-ounce cans
  whole tomatoes
1 1/2 cups juice
  from tomatoes
1 cup water
3/4 cup liquid from clams

1 1/2 teaspoons sugar
1 teaspoon thyme leaves
1/4 teaspoon garlic powder
1/4 teaspoon pepper
7-ounce bottle Dat'l Do-it
  Datil Pepper Hot Sauce*
Four 6 1/2-ounce cans
  chopped clams
2 1/2 cups cooked potatoes,
  cubed

In large pan, cook pork crisp; drain, reserving drippings. Replace 6 Tablespoons drippings in pan with onion, carrot, and celery. Stir over medium heat until tender. Drain and chop tomatoes and stir in with next 7 ingredients; bring to a boil, add hot sauce, cover and simmer 45 minutes. Add clams and potatoes, and heat through. Serves 10 to 12.

*If this sauce, made in St. Augustine, is not available, experiment CAREFULLY with your favorite hot sauce for a similar taste.

TOBY'S CORNER

Even after its admission to the Union in 1845, Florida was isolated; railroads helped populate the state. In Alachua County, a new town established on the Florida Railroad in 1853 was named for General Edmund P. Gaines.

Gainesville prospered from the first, and after the University of Florida opened in 1906, its future was assured. With one of the strongest preservation ordinances in the state, Gainesville has lovely neighborhoods of Victorian-era homes, and in the downtown area, many early structures have been adapted for modern use.

The Gainesville Times was first published in 1876; its successor, combined with the *Alachua Advocate* in the 1880s, was edited and published by Henry H. McCreary as *The Gainesville Daily Sun* until 1917, when it was sold to the Pepper Printing Company. *The Gainesville Sun* remained in the Pepper family until 1962, housed in a 1925 building adjacent to the post office.

The Sun continued publication as part of the Cowles organization until it was purchased by the New York Times Media

Company in 1971. When the paper constructed a new building in 1984, the old *Sun* building was donated to the city; part was altered into offices and shops as the Sun Center, and the oldest portion of the building became Toby's Corner restaurant.

Tastefully decorated in shades of green, Toby's Corner's cozy atmosphere is warm and inviting. Emphasis is on fresh seafood, but the Continental menu also offers veal, beef, lamb, and fowl in a variety of classic preparations. Especially popular are Grouper Madagascar—baked grouper, rolled in Java pepper, in a sauce of cream, Dijon mustard, tomatoes, and brandy— numerous daily specials, and flaming dishes prepared at tableside. Desserts include a superb Key Lime Pie, cheese- cakes, Pecan Walnut Fudge Pie, and well-named Chocolate Heaven.

Toby's Corner, 101 Southeast 2nd Place, Suite 119, Gainesville, is behind the Hippodrome State Theatre, and is open 7 days a week. Lunch, Monday through Friday, is from 11:30 a.m.; dinner, every day, is from 5:30 p.m., with a Sunday Seafood Buffet. (904)375-7620. All legal beverages are served, dress is "dressy casual," and reservations are recommended, especially during football weekends and the Gator National Drag Race. AE,DC,MC,V. ($$$)

TOBY'S CORNER SCALLOPS ORANGE GINGER

1 Tablespoon oil
2 carrots, sliced
1/2 bunch small
  broccoli florets
1/4 pound snow peas,
  strings removed
1 Tablespoon
  minced garlic
1 Tablespoon fresh
  grated ginger

1 1/2 pounds bay scallops
1/4 pound mushrooms,
  quartered
1 Tablespoon orange zest
1/2 cup sherry
Juice of 1 orange
1/2 cup lite soy sauce
Cornstarch
Cooked rice

In large, hot skillet, place oil and sauté next 5 ingredients. Stirring, add next 3 ingredients, then liquids, with cornstarch stirred into a little liquid for thickening. Serve over rice. Serves 4 to 6.

JORDAN'S GROVE

The rolling hills of central Florida were attractive to settlers, but Indians stole their cattle and harbored runaway slaves. Efforts to remove the Indians to western reservations in 1835 caused Seminole Wars that dragged on for 20 years.

A lakeside fort built in 1838 near a lake Indians called "Place of the Muskmelons" was named for Captain William S. Maitland. As the South Florida Railroad came through, villages along its line grew; the town of Lake Maitland was laid out in 1876. Its name was shortened in 1950.

In the 1880s, widespread development of citrus groves supplanted cattle, and huge crops and profits encouraged development until the freeze of 1894-95 killed most of Orange County's citrus trees. New groves were planted, but much of the citrus industry moved south.

A two-story frame house built on an orange grove about 1912 still nestles under a moss-laden live oak on three acres. It was perfect for Mark Rodriguez, 3rd generation restaurateur, to choose as a restaurant in 1984—cozy paneled rooms and the glassed-in porch overlooking gardens are a romantic setting for the amazing creativity of Mark, Clair Epting, and a rotating staff of fellow chefs.

Fresh, organically grown fruits and vegetables and meats grown without steroids or additives are prepared using "Amish to Asian" styles and techniques, on a fixed-price menu that changes daily and includes two courses for lunch and four for dinner.

A memorable meal might include Vidalia Onion and Thyme Soup, Red Snapper Mousseline with Smoked Dolphin Boursin, and Dijon Crusted Organic Roast Pork with Sage/Zinfandel sauce. With a glass of wine from Jordan's Grove's collection, topped off with their justly famous Apple-Blackberry Crisp, you can be as contented as if the grove was your own—and your taste buds will thank you.

Jordan's Grove, 1300 South Orlando Avenue (US 1792), Maitland, is open for a fixed-price two-course lunch Tuesday through Friday and Sunday, 11:30 a.m. to 2:30 p.m. A four-course, fixed price dinner, Tuesday through Saturday, is 6 to 10 p.m. (407)628-0020. Beer, wine, and champagne are available, including many fine wines by the glass; dress is casual to dressy, and reservations are accepted, strongly suggested, especially on weekends and February through May. AE,CB,DC,MC,V. ($$$)

JORDAN'S GROVE
ST. JOHN'S CRAB AND PECAN FRITTERS

2 eggs
2/3 cup dark beer
1 1/2 cups flour
1 teaspoon baking powder
Salt and pepper
1/2 pound lump crab meat

3 Tablespoons
  crushed pecans
1/2 Tablespoon
  minced fresh cilantro
Peanut oil for frying

Beat eggs until light; add next 5 ingredients with a minimum of stirring. Fold in crab meat, pecans, and cilantro. Form batter into fritters using 2 tablespoons. Drop into 425 degree oil and fry until crisp. Serve with your favorite dipping sauce. Serves 6.

COLUMBIA RESTAURANT

Fort Brooke was established on Tampa Bay in 1824 to oversee Indians on their nearby reservation, and the military post was important during the Indian wars.

The town of Tampa grew up around the fort, mushrooming in the 1880s due to several factors: it became a port of entry; the South Florida Railroad reached town, with docking and shipping facilities and owner Henry Plant's palatial Tampa Bay Hotel; deposits of phosphates were discovered nearby; and a fire in Key West caused Vicente Martinez Ybor (pronounced E- bore) to relocate his cigar factory to Tampa.

Other cigar factories helped attract large numbers of workers, mostly Spanish-speaking Cubans, to live and work in Ybor City. Campaigns to free Cuba from Spanish domination began here, with money and guns sent surreptitiously to revolutionists in Cuba, and when the Spanish-American War broke out, Tampa was the primary embarkation port for U.S. troops headed for Cuba.

In 1905, Casimiro Hernandez opened a small corner restaurant in Ybor city; it soon doubled its size, and eventually filled an entire city block, with colorful Spanish tiles and Moorish columns inside and out, and ornate rooms with portraits and crystal chandeliers offset by an interior courtyard surrounded by balconies. As part of the Ybor City Historic District, Columbia Restaurant was placed on the National Register in 1974.

The restaurant, oldest in Florida, has been in the same family for four generations, serving the Spanish and Caribbean specialties that have made it famous. Crusty hot Cuban bread, zesty Ceviche and Gazpacho, several combinations of Paëlla, the freshest Florida seafood, their signature Chicken "Alicante," and superb Sangría keep customers coming back. Classic Spanish and Flamenco Dances are performed six nights a week, creating a cultural experience you'll never forget.

Columbia Restaurant, 2117 East 7th Avenue at 22nd Street, Tampa, may be reached from the 21st Street exit off I-275. It is open 7 days a week, 11 a.m. to 11 p.m. Monday through Saturday, and 12:00 noon to 10 p.m. Sunday. (813)248-4961. All alcoholic beverages are served; most men wear coat and tie January through March; and reservations are suggested. AE,CB,DC,MC,V. ($$)

COLUMBIA SPANISH CARAMEL FLAN

6 Tablespoons sugar   1 cup sugar
4 cups milk   8 eggs
1/8 teaspoon salt   1 teaspoon vanilla

Melt sugar in small skillet until light gold; pour into 1 1/2 quart tube mold and rotate to coat mold. Scald milk with salt, remove from heat and stir in sugar; set aside. In large bowl, beat eggs until foamy. Add milk gradually, then vanilla. Stir well and strain into prepared mold. Set oven at 300 degrees; place mold in shallow pan with hot water halfway up mold and bake 1 hour, or until set. When inserted knife comes out clean, custard is done. Cool, then invert onto serving plate.

THE VERANDA

Driven farther south by each treaty, Indians had retreated to south Florida, where they lived in peace. Cattlemen wanted their grazing lands, however, so Congress offered Indians a bounty to move west, and when they refused, sent in troops.

In early 1850, a fort on the Caloosahatchee River was reactivated and named for Colonel Abraham Myers. It contained 57 buildings, a hospital, lawns, and gardens; supplies and mail were delivered by Manuel Gonzalez in his sloop.

After eight troubled years, Chief Billy Bowlegs surrendered and the fort stood empty, except during the War Between the States, when it was one of four Union forts in Florida.

Captain Gonzalez returned to the fort in 1866 with his five-year-old son Manuel; they repaired a house in the fort while friends went back for wives and household goods. The Gonzalez family operated a trading post on the site of the present Federal Building, and Mrs. Gonzalez was the first teacher in the little community that developed around it.

Young Manuel Gonzalez built two houses at the corner of Second and Broadway. The corner house, built in 1902, was occupied by his daughter Laura and her husband, J.F. Garner; the other was built in 1912. Both houses were purchased by Peter Pulitzer, son of the publisher, and the second house was turned so that its veranda overlooked the courtyard.

Connected by kitchens, the houses are now a restaurant of unusual charm. Chef Dave Ebling's American cuisine features fresh local seafood, Rack of Lamb, and prime beef, with savory soups—marvelous Black Bean in a rich broth—crisp salads with homemade dressings, and fragrant hot oatmeal-honey-molasses bread. Entrées, prepared individually, are generously portioned, and many reflect a Southern influence.

Desserts include fresh berries and cream, Chocolate Pâté, fruit cobblers, and incredible Peanut Butter Fudge Pie—like a half-pound peanut butter cup turned inside out.

The Veranda, 2nd Street at Broadway, Fort Myers, open Monday through Friday for lunch, 11:30 a.m. to 2:30 p.m., and for dinner, 5:30 to 10:30 p.m., Saturday until 11. (813)332-2065. All legal beverages are served, dress is "Dressy Casual," and reservations are recommended. AE,DC,MC,V. ($$$)

THE VERANDA BOURBON STREET FILET

For each serving:
Butter and oil for sautéing
6-ounce tenderloin filet, split into 2 medallions
1/4 cup fresh mushrooms, quartered
1/4 teaspoon fresh garlic, minced
1/4 teaspoon fresh shallots, minced
1/4 cup green onions, chopped
Cracked black pepper
Pinch rosemary
Pinch thyme
3/4 ounce Kentucky sour mash bourbon
1 Tablespoon butter

In sauté pan with small amount of butter and oil, sauté medallions of tenderloin with next 7 ingredients. When it reaches the desired temperature, CAREFULLY flame with bourbon, then finish with butter to smooth the sauce. Do not allow to boil. Medium rare requires about 8 minutes total cooking. Serve medallions on plate; top with sauce.

49

THE BREAKERS

Florida owes much of its growth not only to railroads, but to railroad men. One was Henry M. Flagler, who, with John D. Rockefeller, began Standard Oil. By 1879, the company controlled nearly 95 per cent of the world's oil, and Flagler, at age 50, needed a new challenge.

On his second honeymoon in 1883, Flagler enjoyed St. Augustine so much that he built the $2.5 million Ponce de Leon Hotel—the dining room seated 800—five years later, followed by the Alcazar and the Cordova, all in Spanish Renaissance architecture.

Realizing the wealthy tourists he attracted required better transportation, Flagler bought up short line railroads, improved and extended them, building or renovating plush hotels along the way. By 1888, his railroad reached Daytona, in 1892, New Smyrna, and in 1894, Palm Beach.

Here he built the Royal Poinciana Hotel, his own home, and across Lake Worth, for his many employees, the town of West Palm Beach.

South Florida's first oceanfront hotel, The Palm Beach Inn, was built in 1895, enlarged and renamed "The Breakers" in

1901; destroyed by fire in 1903, its replacement, also of wood, burned in 1925. The final Breakers, built in 1926 by his widow as a memorial to Flagler, was fireproof, with steel girders and hollow tile walls.

Inspired by the Villa Medici in Florence, its twin towers and arcades frame a Florentine fountain, and interiors rival any palazzo. The Breakers was expanded in 1969, and was placed on the National Register in 1973.

In the Florentine Dining Room, beneath an exquisitely painted coffered ceiling, an updated classic cuisine is offered, created from the freshest ingredients. Menus, rotated daily, contain such delights as Medallions of Veal with Foie Gras; Roasted Leg of Wild Young Boar; Fruit Filled Pork Loin in Puff Pastry; and selections of fresh Florida fish, creatively prepared.

The Breakers attentive service is never pompous; the atmosphere is one of unrestrained elegance; an orchestra plays for listening and dancing; and the food is grand.

What more could anyone ask?

The Florentine Dining Room at The Breakers, South County Road, Palm Beach, is open 7 days a week. Breakfast, buffet and à la carte, is 7 to 11 a.m.; dinner is 6:30 to 10 p.m. It is not open for lunch. (407)655-6611. All beverages are served, including one of the country's largest wine collections; jacket and tie are required during the "season," and jackets on all Sundays; reservations are recommended. AE,CB,DC,MC,V. ($$$)

THE BREAKERS RACK OF LAMB DIJONNAISE*

1 rack of lamb, split in half   2 cups herbed
4 Tablespoons   bread crumbs
  Dijon mustard
2 teaspoons
  red wine vinegar

Sear the racks and set aside. When cool, dip in mustard/vinegar mix, then in bread crumbs. Place on roasting tray and roast about 17 minutes at 350 degrees. Serves 4.

*From the forthcoming BREAKERS COOKBOOK.
Used by permission.

CAP'S PLACE ISLAND RESTAURANT

During Prohibition years, Florida's extensive coastline tempted "bootleggers" and "rumrunners," who smuggled illegal alcoholic beverages into the country. Just outside territorial waters, large ships laden with contraband awaited smaller craft that ferried liquor into hidden inlets. Both speedboats (often armed) and innocent-looking fishing vessels were used, and the undermanned Coast Guard was hard pressed to stop the traffic.

Gambling, too, was illegal in Florida, although plush clubs were discreetly operated in resort areas. Both these facts meant profit for Captain Eugene "Cap" Knight, a fisherman who lived on a grounded dredging barge in a mangrove swamp north of Ft. Lauderdale. He turned his home into a speakeasy/casino/restaurant accessible only by water, and his brother, lighthouse keeper on the point, signaled when the wrong people headed up the inlet.

The simple rustic buildings of Cap's Place have been nominated for inclusion on the National Register.

When prohibition was over, Cap maintained a seafood restaurant beloved by residents and winter visitors alike. He lived until he was nearly 92, and had already turned the restaurant over to longtime bartender Al Hassis and his wife Pat, whose three children operate the restaurant today.

Cap's Place still provides the fresh seafood that made it famous. You choose which kind, the method of preparation (broiled, sautéed, pan fried, etc.), the sauce (Dijon, Cajun, Creamy Dill), and accompaniments. Just don't miss the Manhattan-Style Grouper Chowder and the remarkable Fresh Hearts of Palm Salad.

And you can still look forward to the all-too-brief boat ride back to the dock.

Cap's Place Island Restaurant, 2765 Northeast 28th Court, Lighthouse Point, is open for dinner 7 days a week, 5:30 to 10 p.m., to 11 Friday and Saturday. Just north of Pompano Beach, it is hard to find on your first visit: off I-95, take East Copans Road to US 1, then north two traffic lights to Northeast 24th Street. Turn east, and follow green and white Cap's Place signs to dock. (305)941-0418. All beverages are served, dress is casual (take a jacket for warmth), and reservations are accepted. AE,MC,V. ($$)

CAP'S PLACE BLUEFISH DIJON

For each serving:
1 filet of bluefish
 (or other fish)
Lemon juice

2 Tablespoons
 Dijon Sauce*
Margarine

Marinate filet in lemon juice about 10 minutes. Dip fish in Dijon Sauce and place, skin side up, in heavy skillet that has been greased with margarine. Cook over medium heat about 5 minutes, or until no longer translucent. Turn, spread with Dijon Sauce, and cook an additional few minutes.

*For Dijon Sauce: Whisk together 1/2 cup Dijon mustard, 1 cup liquid margarine, 1 teaspoon minced fresh garlic, 1 Tablespoon lemon juice, and 1 teaspoon paprika. Yields enough for 8 servings; may also be used on chicken.

GEORGIA

1. CLARKESVILLE
   Glen-Ella Springs Inn
2. ATHENS
   Trumps at the Georgian
3. ROSWELL
   La Grotta
4. MARIETTA
   The Planters
5. ATLANTA
   The Abbey
6. AUGUSTA
   The Partridge Inn
7. MACON
   Victorian Village Bistro
8. SAVANNAH
   The Olde Pink House Restaurant
   Elizabeth on 37th
9. JEKYLL ISLAND
   Jekyll Island Club

GLEN-ELLA SPRINGS INN

Habersham County was named for colorful patriot Joseph Habersham, Postmaster General under our first three Presidents. One of the first Savannah residents to summer in the North Georgia mountains, Habersham built a house near Clarkesville; by the 1830s, the area was a popular resort.

Adjacent to Glen and Ella Davidson's 1875 farmhouse, a house built in 1890 accommodated paying guests. In 1905, the two were connected, creating a sprawling frame hotel with 2-story porches. Ella's food and a "healing" spring assured the success of the hotel, which remained in operation until the 1920s, and in the family until the 1950s.

It had deteriorated when Bobby and Barrie Aycock bought it in 1986, but Bobby restored heart pine interiors and found hidden fieldstone fireplaces; only porches needed replacing, and electricity and plumbing were installed for the first time. The Glen-Ella Springs Inn opened in 1987, and was placed on the National Register in 1990.

Cozy fires, comfortable furnishings, and Barrie's "sophisticated American and Continental" cuisine again attract guests to feast on fresh mountain trout, local fruits and vegetables, and homemade breads and desserts.

For lunch, try corn chowder and her famous chicken salad, or perhaps the 6-ounce burger; dinner includes bacon-wrapped scallops, Cajun specialties, rack of lamb, and prime rib. Save room for homemade pies (Apple Streusel, Key Lime), cheesecake, or Chocolate Indulgence, and take time to relax on the porch and study the mountains across the meadow.

Glen-Ella Springs Inn, near Turnerville, between Clarkesville and Clayton, Georgia, is 1 1/2 miles off US 441 on Bear Gap Road. June 1 to December 31 it is open Tuesday through Sunday; lunch is 12:00 noon to 2 p.m., dinner 6 to 9 p.m., and Sunday Brunch Buffet 11 a.m. to 2 p.m. Winter hours vary; it is open weekends, plus dinner Wednesday through Saturday. (404)754-7295; (800)552-3479. Dress is casual, reservations are strongly suggested (a MUST for weekend dinner), and busiest time is "Leaf Season" in Autumn. There are 16 overnight units. AE,MC,V. ($$)

GLEN-ELLA SPRINGS BRAN SCONES

1 3/4 cups flour
1 1/2 teaspoons
  baking powder
1/2 teaspoon baking soda
1/4 cup sugar
6 Tablespoons cold butter,
  cubed

2 Tablespoons
  heavy cream
1/2 cup buttermilk
1/3 cup All Bran cereal
2 teaspoons heavy cream
1 Tablespoon sugar

In large bowl, combine first 4 ingredients; cut in butter until mealy. In small bowl, combine next 3 ingredients. Mix with flour until dough masses together. On floured surface, pat out 3/4" thick, cut into 2-inch rounds. Place on greased baking sheet, brush with cream and sprinkle with sugar. Bake 20 minutes at 350 degrees, until golden brown. If freezing, do not brown; cool and wrap tightly. Thaw and reheat until brown. Yields 16.

TRUMPS at THE GEORGIAN

Chartered in 1785, the University of Georgia actually began in 1801, when John Milledge, later Governor, donated 633 acres overlooking the Oconee River for the school and a town.

Juxtaposition of town and gown benefited both; Athens became the commercial center of Northeast Georgia, and the college was a true university by the first quarter of the 20th century.

Although early visitors to the University and business travelers stayed at a number of small hotels, by 1908, Athens, with a population of 10,000, needed a new hotel.

At a cost of $200,000, the impressive 5-story brick Georgian Hotel was constructed on the highest ridge in Clarke County, and boasted a marble lobby, stained glass windows and skylights, and running water in every room. For generations, it hosted social, business, and political functions; as part of the Downtown Historic District, it was placed on the National Register in 1978.

The hotel operation ceased in 1976; in 1985, it was rehabilitated as an apartment building, The Georgian, and in 1987, Helene and Ron Schwartz and Andree Kosak moved their successful restaurant, Trumps, into the marble lobby.

Elegant, comfortable surroundings enhance "good, fresh food" prepared to order in a contemporary Continental manner. Fresh ingredients are treated with a light touch and interesting sauces; more unusual items appear as specials—Chicken Feta, with scallions and black olives, baked Mozzarella with marinara sauce, Tempura chicken tenderloin with cherry-mustard dressing.

Trumps' most popular dessert is chocolate chip pecan pie, but they also offer cheesecakes, homemade cinnamon ice cream, Double Chocolate Torte, and White Chocolate Deluxe: Chocolate cookie crust and dark chocolate cheesecake, topped with white chocolate mousse.

Trumps at The Georgian, 247 East Washington Street, Athens, is open for lunch Monday through Friday, 11 a.m. to 2:30 p.m., for dinner Monday through Thursday 5 to 10 p.m., until 11 Friday and Saturday. Sunday dinner is 6 to 11 p.m.; Sunday brunch, September to mid-June, is 10 a.m. to 2 p.m. (404)546-6388. All legal beverages are served, dress is "casual and up," and reservations are suggested. Busiest times are Georgia football games. AE,MC,V. ($$)

TRUMPS HONEY-BOURBON CHICKEN

4 Boneless chicken breasts
Flour, seasoned with
** Salt and pepper**
CLARIFIED butter or
** margarine for sautéing**

Honey-Bourbon Sauce*
Chopped pecans
Chopped green tops
** of scallion**

Dredge chicken breasts in flour; sauté, and set aside.

*For sauce: Measure 1/2 cup honey and 1/2 cup bourbon. Heat bourbon over high heat (carefully) to burn off alcohol. Add honey and continue to heat. Thicken, if needed, with arrowroot or cornstarch. Pour over chicken and sprinkle with pecans and scallion tops. Serves 4.

LA GROTTA

R̲oswell King, of Darien, near
Savannah, selected a town site on the Chattahoochee River in
1829; in 1837, he relocated and built a cotton mill. With family
and friends, he established a town characterized by fine Greek
Revival houses; one of these, Bulloch Hall, was the childhood
home of Mittie Bulloch, mother of President Theodore Roosevelt
and grandmother of Eleanor Roosevelt.

Over-farmed cotton land caused a depression in mid-19th
century, and Roswell, further damaged by Union occupation
and vandalism during the War Between the States, was slow to
recover. The mill, burned by Federals, was rebuilt, but the town
never regained its industrial prominence.

Prior to 1874, a hip-roofed frame cottage was built north of
Roswell's square for a Dr. Grier; according to local tradition, it
was constructed by three brothers who owed him money. He
lived and practiced medicine there until his death, stabling
horses in the basement. As part of the Roswell Historic District,
it was placed on the National Register in 1974.

Sergio Favalli, Chef Antonio Pecondon, and Gildo Fusinaz,
partners in Atlanta's successful La Grotta restaurant, chose the

house for a second location in 1981. Decorated in shades of rose and peach, with enclosed porches overlooking a 150-year-old tree, La Grotta specializes in Northern Italian cuisine, with fresh pastas and rich cream sauces.

Each dish is prepared to order, using the finest ingredients—fresh fish; milk-fed veal; tomatoes, sausages, and cheeses from New York—combined in traditional recipes with a modern flair. Desserts, especially Trifle, Tira Misù, and a velvety Crème Brûlée, top off an outstanding meal.

La Grotta Ristorante, 647 Atlanta Street, Roswell, is just North of the square, and is open Tuesday through Saturday, 6 to 10:30 p.m.; weekend seatings are at 7 and 9 p.m. (404)998-0645. All legal beverages are served, most men wear jacket and tie, and reservations are preferred. It is closed the last two weeks in July. AE,DC,DS,MC,V. ($$$)

LA GROTTA CARPACCIO

1 pound beef tenderloin
1 1/2 teaspoons
 chopped fresh sage
1 1/2 teaspoons
 chopped fresh basil
1 1/2 teaspoons
 chopped Italian parsley
1/2 cup chopped shallots

1 Tablespoon
 Dijon mustard
Juice of one lemon
1 1/4 cups olive oil
2 Tablespoons
 red wine vinegar
Salt and pepper

Trim tenderloin, removing all fat and membrane. Freeze briefly, then slice very thin. Place in non-reactive container. In bowl, combine next 6 ingredients; whisk rapidly while adding oil and vinegar by drops. Season to taste. Pour over beef and marinate at least 4 hours. Serves 6.

THE PLANTERS

During the hot summer of 1864, fierce battles raged from Chattanooga southward, as badly outnumbered Confederate forces retreated toward Atlanta, pursued by relentless General W. T. Sherman.

One of the few antebellum structures left in their wake is a plantation house built about 1848 by John Heyward Glover, the first mayor of Marietta. During the Atlanta campaign, "Bushy Park" was occupied by William King, a son of Roswell's founder, whose prior acquaintance with Sherman is credited with its survival.

An extraordinary example of Greek Revival style, the house has a pedimented 4-column Doric portico overlooking 13 acres remaining from the original 3,000. Enlarged and remodeled in 1939, it was placed on the National Register in 1977, and was restored in 1979 to become The Planters restaurant.

Inside, its wide staircase hall, high ceilings, and antiques—some original to the house—recall the graciousness of the Old South.

The Planters' food also has a feeling of Southern expansiveness. The 5-course meal provides at least 3 choices each of appetizers, soups, salads, and desserts, and nine or more of entrées; price is determined by entrées, which include fresh vegetables and wonderful homemade breads.

Chef Ron Simoneau, who has been with The Planters since its beginning, and his wife Melissa, pastry chef, produce a sophisticated menu that changes seasonally. Your meal might include Sautéed Lump Crab Cakes in Lime Herb Butter as appetizer; Pumpkin Soup with Pheasant and Toasted Pumpkin Seeds; Mushroom and Artichoke Salad; Roast Boneless Duckling with Raspberry-Orange Sauce; and Papaya Coconut Tart with Macaroon Crust.

As you dine, watch the shadows lengthen on the lawn and dream of a way of life which, if it ever existed, is certainly gone with the wind.

The Planters, 780 South Cobb Drive, Marietta, is 4.3 miles west from I-75 exit 111 (Lockheed-Dobbins); entrance is on the right. It is open for a fixed-price, 5-course dinner Monday through Saturday, weeknights from 6:30 p.m., Friday and Saturday from 6 p.m. (404)427-4646. Most men wear coat and tie, reservations are recommended, and all legal beverages are served. AE,CB,DC,DS,MC,V ($$$).

THE PLANTERS GIN AND TOMATO SOUP

21 ounces canned
  whole tomatoes
10 ounces canned
  tomato sauce
1 Tablespoon paprika
1/2 teaspoon dried thyme
1/4 teaspoon salt
1 1/2 Tablespoons sugar
1/4 teaspoon black pepper
3/4 teaspoon
  chopped garlic

5 ounces gin
3 ounces heavy cream
5 ounces bacon, cooked,
  drained, and crumbled
4 ounces julienned
  shiitake mushrooms,
  sautéed
3 tablespoons
  softened butter

In large saucepan, combine first 8 ingredients. Bring to a boil, reduce heat, and simmer 1 to 1 1/2 hours. Add gin, simmer 30 minutes, add cream, blend and strain. Stir in remaining ingredients and serve. Do not allow to boil. Serves 4.

THE ABBEY

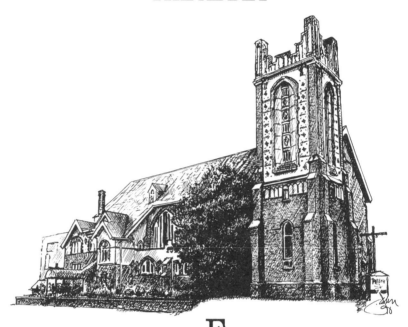

From mid-July to mid-August, 1864, Atlanta lay under siege, bombarded by Sherman's artillery. Confederate forces left the city September 1, burning munitions trains behind them; the Union army evacuated civilians, then set fire to the remaining buildings November 14, when they departed on the infamous march to the sea.

Atlanta was destroyed, but like its symbol, The Phoenix, rose from the ashes immediately. Within three years, it was again capital of Georgia, railroads were back in operation, and its population had returned and increased. Constantly changing, never finished, Atlanta remains a testament to the vitality of the New South.

By 1918, a massive dark-brick structure occupied the southwest corner of Ponce de Leon and Piedmont Avenues. The Ponce de Leon Avenue Methodist church featured a rectangular tower, gothic windows and arches, and impressive stained-glass windows. It was vacated in 1944, and, after remaining empty several years, housed congregations from other denominations.

In 1977, Bill Swearingen relocated his well-established restaurant, The Abbey, in the former church, enhancing the ecclesiastical atmosphere with tapestry, artwork, and waiters in monk's garb. Tall brass candlesticks and a harpist in the balcony add to the effect, but the fare is far from monastic.

Under the direction of George Gore, The Abbey's long-time staff of 100 produces fine contemporary Continental and American food. Everything—ice creams, pastries, pastas—is made on the premises, meats are hand-cut daily, and guests may observe the kitchen staff at work through a large window.

Especially noteworthy here are such entrées as Smoked Salmon with Wild Mushroom Sauce, Roast Duck with Figs in Fresh Applesauce, and the famous Rack of Lamb. Fresh fish and game are available year-round, and unusual desserts include Apples Baked in Custard Layered with Macadamia Nut Brittle, Chocolate Fig Cognac Torte with Hazelnuts, and Pumpkin Bread Pudding with Caramel Sauce.

The Abbey, 163 Ponce de Leon Avenue, Atlanta, is open for dinner 7 days a week, with seatings every 15 minutes from 6 to 10 p.m. (404) 876-8532. All legal beverages are served, "cosmopolitan attire" is worn, and reservations are suggested. AE,CB,DC,DS,MC,V. ($$$)

THE ABBEY CRÈME DE BRIE

2 ounces butter
1 pound onions, diced
1/4 teaspoon diced garlic
1/2 pound mushrooms,
  sliced
1 cup dry white wine
2 ounces flour
3 1/2 cups chicken stock
1 bay leaf

Pinch chopped
  fresh thyme
2 1/2 cups whipping cream
10 ounces sliced
  brie cheese, divided
Salt and pepper
Scant 2 ounces sherry
12 slices French bread,
  toasted

In large pan, melt butter; sauté next three ingredients. Add wine; reduce until almost dry, then stir in flour. Add stock and bay leaf, bring to boil, and cook until thickened. Add thyme and cream, strain, and replace on burner; slowly whisk in 6 ounces brie until smooth. Season and stir in sherry. Pour into bowls, cover with toasts, then top with remaining cheese and broil lightly. Serves 6.

THE PARTRIDGE INN

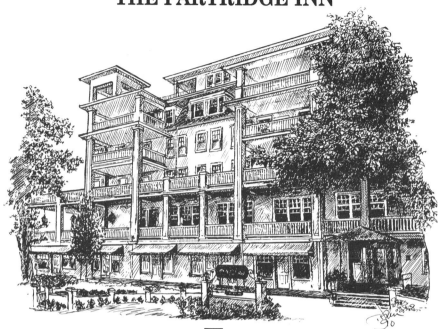

The town of Augusta, authorized by Georgia Trustees in 1736, was built 150 miles up river from Savannah. Near an Indian trading post, Georgia's second town became an early commercial center.

After bitter fighting and siege during the Revolution, Augusta served as Georgia's first Capital, 1785 to 1795; during this period, prominent Georgians, including Governor John Milledge and George Walton, built homes in the sand hills above town.

"Summerville," benefited from a climate thought to prevent yellow fever. A summer retreat for social Southerners, it acquired electric lights, stores, and hotels when wealthy Northerners came for winters in the late 1800s.

About 1900, Morris Partridge bought a 2-story 1870s Summerville residence for a small hotel that expanded five times; in 1929, The Partridge Inn had 129 rooms. It hosted social events for generations, but deteriorated after World War II, and became an apartment house in the 1960s.

As part of the Summerville Historic District, the building was placed on the National Register in 1980. Threatened with demolition, it was rescued by a $6 million dollar rehabilitation, and in 1988 again became an elegant hotel, known for outstanding food.

In the crisp white and mauve second-floor dining room, wide windows open onto verandas overlooking the city, and fresh local ingredients create an updated Southern cuisine. Hot popovers precede such clever twists as Grits Soufflé, Crisp Duck with Augusta Peaches, and Broiled Turkey Breast with Black-eyed Peas. Luscious desserts include Chocolate Bread Pudding, homemade ice creams, and Pecan Tart with Whiskey Sauce.

The Partridge Inn, 2110 Walton Way, Augusta, is open 7 days a week. Breakfast is 6:30 a.m. to 10:30 a.m.; lunch and Sunday brunch buffet are 11:30 a.m. to 2:30 p.m.; afternoon tea, Monday through Saturday, is 3 to 5 p.m.; dinner is 5:30 to 10 p.m., to 11 p.m. Friday and Saturday. (404)737-8888, (800)476-6888. All legal beverages are served, most men wear coat and tie, and reservations are requested, a necessity during The Masters golf tournament, 1st week in April. There are 105 overnight units. AE,CB,DC,MC,V. ($$)

PARTRIDGE INN CRAB IN PHYLLO PASTRY

Filling:
10 ounces crab meat
1 teaspoon diced
  red bell peppers
1 teaspoon diced
  green bell peppers
1 teaspoon diced tomatoes
2 teaspoons finely
  sliced scallions

1 teaspoon
  chopped parsley
Salt and pepper
Cayenne pepper or
  hot green pepper sauce
1 ounce heavy cream

Mix all ingredients together.

Wrapping: 3 ounces melted butter
4 sheets phyllo pastry or
thin puff pastry

Brush each pastry sheet with butter, fold in half lengthwise, place 1/4 of filling in center of sheet, roll up and twist ends (like a candy wrapper). Brush with butter, place on baking pan and bake 8 to 10 minutes, or until golden. Serve with a white wine or shrimp cream sauce. Serves 4.

VICTORIAN VILLAGE BISTRO

Prehistoric Indians had farmed the area where the fall line crosses the Ocmulgee River, Spaniards with de Soto had passed through, and it was an important site in dealing with Creek Indians, but permanent European settlement did not come until early 19th Century.

Macon, laid out in 1823, grew rapidly into a trading center and inland port, linked by flatboats with the Eastern Seaboard. By 1829 there were 2000 inhabitants, and the coming of steamboats and railways assured its future. A Confederate arsenal and treasury, the town was threatened by Federal forces during the War Between the States, but never captured. It surrendered peacefully in 1865.

Slow recovery after the war was followed by industrial and residential growth, during which Macon sprawled westward. Among the handsome Queen Anne-style houses built on Hardeman Avenue around the turn of the century are several which were restored in 1988 to begin "Victorian Village."

The growing complex of beautifully restored buildings so far includes an inn with rooms in four "gingerbread" houses, an amphitheater, and the Victorian Village Bistro. A cluster of period cottages awaits restoration.

The 2-story frame house at the corner of Pursley was built before the 1870s and enlarged several times. Isaac Hardeman raised a family in it, then deeded it to his daughter Roberta when she married George S. Jones in the 1890s; the house's second story and a two-story addition were built during the Jones occupancy. It achieved its present appearance by 1924, and is now the Victorian Village Bistro.

Guests may enjoy a drink on the wraparound porch before dinner in the rose and green dining rooms, where fine Continental food is presented.

Favorites here include Beef Wellington, Scampi, Veal Marsala, and Fettuccine Alfredo, with special nightly features. There's a variety of tempting desserts—Key Lime Pie is good—but don't miss the spectacular flaming citrus coffee!

Victorian Village Bistro, 1875 Hardeman Avenue, Macon, is open for lunch Monday through Friday, 11:30 a.m. to 2:30 p.m., and for dinner Monday through Saturday 5:30 to 10:30 p.m. (912)745-1288. Victorian Village Inn has 31 overnight units in 4 historic buildings. (912)743-3333. AE,MC,V. ($$)

VICTORIAN VILLAGE
SHRIMP AND SCALLOPS TARRAGON

2 teaspoons
  chopped shallots
2 Tablespoons
  tarragon leaves
1/2 cup white wine
8 large shrimp,
  peeled and deveined

8 to 10 sea scallops
1/2 cup heavy cream
1 chicken-flavored
  bouillon cube
2 teaspoons roux*

In saucepan, place first 3 ingredients and bring to a boil; add shrimp and scallops and poach until half of liquid remains. Add cream and bouillon cube. When almost boiling, add roux and simmer until thick. Serves 1.

*For roux: rub 1 Tablespoon flour and 1 Tablespoon soft butter into a paste.

THE OLDE PINK HOUSE RESTAURANT

J ames Edward Oglethorpe, appalled by English debtors' prisons, petitioned George II to charter a 13th colony in which bankrupt people could start a new life producing silks, wines, and spices for English consumption.

On February 12, 1733, 125 people, few of them actually debtors, landed at a high bluff on the Savannah River. The town they laid out, with wide shady streets and garden-like squares, was one of the first planned cities in North America, and remains one of the most beautiful.

Georgia's Sons of Liberty included three sons of early settler James Habersham: Joseph, John, and James. It was James who built the handsome two-story, Georgian-style house on Reynolds Square. Of brick covered with stucco, the house acquired its color when the brick bled through. In 1812, it became The Planters' Bank; it was altered and enlarged, and vaults were built in the basement. The Greek revival portico was added about 1820.

Preservation came to Savannah in the 1950s, and most of the town's old buildings were saved and restored. The entire Savannah Historic District was named a National Historic

Landmark in 1966.

The Habersham house had deteriorated with time, although it had remained in use as lawyers' offices and a long-lived tea room, with a bookstore in the basement. In 1970, it was painstakingly restored, and opened as the Olde Pink House Restaurant in 1971.

Today, delectable "Low Country" and Southern foods are served in four handsomely appointed dining rooms. You might feast on Ogeechee Mull (shrimp, chicken, and ham in a tomato sauce), Veal Thomas Jefferson, or fresh local seafood before sampling such desserts as Sherry Trifle and Black Bottom Pie.

The Olde Pink House, 23 Abercorn Street, Savannah, is open 7 days a week. Lunch is 11:30 a.m. to 2:30 p.m., Monday through Saturday, and dinner is 5:30 to 10:30 p.m. (912)232-4286. All legal beverages are served, most men wear coats for dinner, and reservations are preferred. AE,MC,V. ($$$)

OLDE PINK HOUSE ANN'S
PEANUT BUTTER PIE*

One 9-inch baked pie crust	1/4 cup cornstarch
1/2 cup creamy	2 cups milk, scalded
peanut butter	2 Tablespoons butter
1 cup powdered sugar	1 teaspoon vanilla
3 egg yolks	1 cup heavy cream,
2/3 cup sugar	whipped with
1/8 teaspoon salt	1 Tablespoon sugar

Blend peanut butter and powdered sugar in small bowl; set aside. Place yolks in top of double boiler over hot (not boiling) water; beat until fluffy. Combine next three ingredients, beat into yolks, add milk and heat until smooth and thick. Remove from heat; add butter and vanilla. Spread 2/3 of peanut butter mixture in bottom of pie shell; pour hot custard over, and cool. Spread whipped cream on pie and crumble remaining peanut butter mixture on top.

*From RECIPES FROM THE OLDE PINK HOUSE Copyright© 1981 McCallar and Keith, Savannah, Georgia. Used by permission.

ELIZABETH ON 37th

The American Revolution in Georgia was a messy guerrilla war. Strikes against opposing sides were made by quasimilitary groups with personal grudges, factions within Continental forces squabbled among themselves, and ineptly defended Savannah fell almost without resistance.

Eighty-two years later, Sherman made his land-scorching march to the sea, and Savannah, blockaded for two years, again capitulated. An advantage was the relatively light damage sustained by the city and a peaceful occupation, with a quick recovery after reconstruction.

Savannah grew to the south after the War, and about 1900, the Gibbes family, successful cotton brokers, built a home on 37th Street patterned after one seen in Boston. With some elements of Beaux Arts and Italian Renaissance styles, the 2-story stucco house is an impressive corner landmark.

Elizabeth and Michael Terry, seeking a less hectic life than Atlanta offered, bought the house in 1980 and remodeled it to include living quarters upstairs and a restaurant down. A welcoming fireplace in the spacious hall and unpretentious decor make this serious restaurant a comfortable place to be.

Elizabeth's original concept, with a simple menu of broiled and sautéed dishes, grew, by customer request, to include more and more elaborate food. Fresh regional foods are imaginatively combined—Grilled Quail and Shrimp with Savannah Red Rice, Baked Crab Cakes with Corn-Hominy Relish—with daily appetizer and entrée specials, and as many as ten extravagantly rich, beautifully presented desserts.

Elizabeth on 37th, 105 East 37th Street, Savannah, is open Monday through Saturday for dinner, 6 to 10:30 p.m. (912)236-5547. All legal beverages are served, most men wear coat and tie, reservations are recommended, especially for Saturdays. The restaurant is closed 2 weeks in August. AE,MC,V. ($$$)

ELIZABETH ON 37th
GRILLED SHRIMP AND CHERRY TOMATOES
WITH PEANUT GRILLING SAUCE

12 8-inch rosemary sticks or bamboo skewers
2 pounds 21-25 count shrimp, peeled and deveined
18 cherry tomatoes
1 large onion, in 1" pieces
Fresh bay leaves or fresh mint leaves
1/4 cup vegetable oil
2 Tablespoons minced fresh thyme
1 teaspoon fresh cracked pepper
Peanut Grilling Sauce*

Skewer first 4 ingredients. Combine oil, thyme, and pepper; brush over kabobs and hold at room temperature 1 hour before grilling. Pre-heat grill; reduce flame to low or allow coals to become white; set rack at highest level.

Brush kabobs with marinade again and grill 2 minutes; turn and brush with Peanut Grilling Sauce on second side. Grill about 2 minutes; shrimp should be pink. Pass remaining sauce with kabobs. Serves 6.

*For Peanut Grilling Sauce: In food processor or small bowl, combine 1/3 cup peanut butter, 1 Tablespoon soy sauce, 1/2 teaspoon chili oil, 1 teaspoon sesame oil, juice of 1/2 lemon, 1/2 Tablespoon minced elephant garlic, and 1/2 cup chicken or vegetable broth. Mix well and refrigerate; sauce will be thin, but will thicken in 1 hour.

JEKYLL ISLAND CLUB

Captain William Horton, under orders from General Oglethorpe, established an outpost on Jekyll in 1736. Spanish troops, retreating after the Battle of Bloody Marsh in 1742, burned Horton's house, but he rebuilt and lived on the island until 1748.

In 1886, Jekyll became a club for such industrialists as Vincent Astor, Marshall Field, J. P. Morgan, Joseph Pulitzer, and William Vanderbilt. Some members of the Jekyll Island Club built individual "cottages," but many stayed in the turreted Club House.

With a dairy, garden, laundry, library, and church, the island provided all comforts; members and guests enjoyed riding, cycling, tennis, hunting, picnicking and golf.

Difficulties caused by the Depression were compounded by World War II shortages, and the club closed in 1942. Purchased by the state of Georgia in 1947, Jekyll Island is a popular state park. Many "cottages" have been restored, and the 240-acre Jekyll Island Club Historic District was declared a National Historic Landmark in 1978.

The Club House, renovated and enlarged in 1987, is a

luxury hotel. Beneath the Grand Dining Room's gleaming white columns, guests savor individually prepared dishes emphasizing fresh seafoods and regional favorites with a variety of special sauces. Beautifully presented, in an atmosphere of relaxed elegance, these meals make everyone feel like a millionaire in the golden era of The Jekyll Island Club.

The Jekyll Island Club, a Radisson Resort, is open 7 days a week. In the Grand Dining Room, breakfast is 6:30 to 11 a.m., to 10 a.m. Sunday; lunch is 11:30 a.m. to 2 p.m., Monday through Saturday; Sunday brunch is 10:30 a.m. to 2 p.m.; dinner is 5:30 to 10 p.m. (912)635-2600, (800)822-1886. All legal beverages are served, including Sunday—after 12:30 p.m. Dress is casual, coats and ties preferred for dinner; and reservations are expected for dinner. There are 134 overnight units in 3 historic buildings. AE,CB,DC,DS,MC,V. ($$$)

JEKYLL ISLAND CLUB VENISON SIR JEKYLL

1 ounce pecan pieces	2 ounces flour
2 ounces peanuts	for dredging
1/2 teaspoon	1 large egg, beaten
ground cinnamon	1 ounce oil for sautéing
1/2 cup bread crumbs	Sauce*
5 ounces	
venison scaloppine	

In food processor, place first four ingredients and process to fine crumbs. Dredge scaloppine in flour, dip in egg, then dredge in crumb mixture. Place oil in hot sauté pan and brown scaloppine on one side; turn and cook 2 to 4 minutes in 400 degree oven. Top with sauce. Serves 1.

*For sauce: In hot sauté pan, place 2 ounces butter. Sauté 2 mushrooms, sliced; 1/2 ounce diced tomatoes; 1/2 ounce julienned smoked ham; and 1 Tablespoon chopped parsley. Deglaze pan with 1 ounce white wine and 2 ounces demi-glaze or brown gravy. Remove from fire and whisk in 2 ounces butter.

KENTUCKY

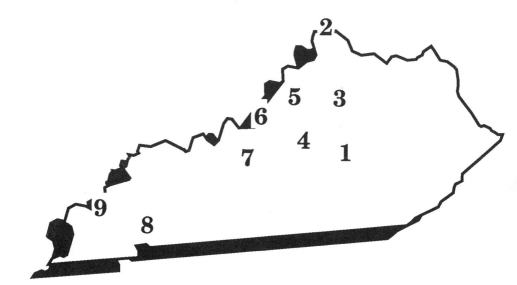

1. BEREA
   Boone Tavern
2. COVINGTON
   Dee Felice Café
3. LEXINGTON
   Dudley's Restaurant
4. HARRODSBURG
   Beaumont Inn
   Shaker Village of Pleasant Hill
5. SHELBYVILLE
   Science Hill Inn
6. ANCHORAGE
   Train Station Restaurant
7. GLENDALE
   The Whistle Stop Restaurant
8. HOPKINSVILLE
   Bartholomew's
9. PADUCAH
   The Ninth Street House

BOONE TAVERN

Berea College began in 1855 as a non-sectarian, interracial school for needy Appalachian children. Today, 1500 students, mostly from the Southern Appalachians, benefit from Berea's work-study program.

Every student works at least 10 hours a week while carrying a full academic load, defraying all or part of their fees; tuition is guaranteed, supported by endowment and gifts. Berea Student Industries are a source of income for the college, and high-quality student crafts are available in college shops and through catalog sales.

About 150 Berea students work in the Boone Tavern Hotel and Dining Room, which was opened in 1909 as a guest house for the college, and rapidly became a popular stopover. Expanded in 1928, the three-story Georgian-style building covers most of a city block, and is furnished with antique reproduction furniture from Student Industries. The dining room's many-paned windows overlook the campus, and the atmosphere is one of homelike comfort.

Richard T. Hougen, Manager of Boone Tavern from 1940 to 1976, established and headed the Hotel Management Department at Berea College. During his tenure he wrote three cookbooks which formed the basis for Boone Tavern's updated Southern cuisine. His recipes are still used, and the books are available in the lobby.

Fresh regional foods, often purchased from local farmers, are cleverly seasoned and attractively presented. Each meal comes with appetizer, salad, entrée, fresh vegetables and dessert, plus relishes at dinner. Two wonderful hot breads are passed (the spoon bread, served only at dinner, is legendary); for dessert, rich Jefferson Davis Pie and Black Forest Cake contrast with Grapefruit Sherbet and Island Coconut Ice Cream.

Boone Tavern, Berea, is open 7 days a week. Breakfast is 7 to 9 a.m., lunch 11:30 a.m. to 1:30 p.m., and dinner 6 to 7:30 p.m. Lunch on Sundays and holidays is 12 noon to 2 p.m. (606)986-9358. Berea is 40 miles south of Lexington, just east of I-75. Coats for men and tailored attire for women are required in the evening, and reservations are requested, essential on weekends in April and October. There are 57 overnight units, and there is a strict no-tipping policy. AE,DC,DS,MC,V. ($$)

BOONE TAVERN JEFFERSON DAVIS PIE*

One 9-inch
  unbaked pie shell
2 cups brown sugar
1 Tablespoon sifted flour
1/2 teaspoon nutmeg
1 cup cream
4 eggs, slightly beaten

1 teaspoon lemon juice
1/2 teaspoon grated
  lemon rind
1/4 cup melted margarine
Whipped cream
  for garnish

Sift sugar with flour and nutmeg; add cream and mix well. Blend in eggs, add lemon juice, rind, and margarine. Beat well. Pour into pie shell and bake 45 minutes at 375 degrees. Cool and serve with whipped cream. Serves 8.

*From COOKING WITH HOUGEN. Copyright1960 Richard T. Hougen, Berea, Kentucky. Used by permission.

DEE FELICE CAFÉ

During the period of western expansion, many German immigrants floated down the Ohio River to settle in the bustling little city of Covington. Newcomers included artisans of all types, merchants, industrialists, and professionals.

In 1868, builder James G. Arnold erected a 3-story building at the northwest corner of Main and 6th streets, housing businesses at street level, and a meeting hall above. Edward L. Pieck, a Covington native of German extraction, opened his pharmacy in the corner store in 1885.

By 1890, Pieck had expanded into the center store, opening the wall with slender columns. Pictures at that time show a molded tin ceiling and a marble floor, with a cast iron storefront; few changes have been made, although two elegant rooms, with stained glass windows, a tented ceiling, and oak mantels, were added at the rear around the turn of the century. The building remained a pharmacy until 1971, and as part of the West Side/Main Strasse Historic District, it was placed on the National Register in 1983.

Dee Felice, a jazz musician and band leader who has

performed with Mel Torme, Julius La Rosa, James Brown, and Sergio Mendez, opened his jazz club and restaurant in two corner stores in 1984, carefully maintaining its Victorian flavor. The third store has been included, with arches into the main room where jazz is played nightly on a stage behind the bar.

Guests enjoy the blend of foods on the menu: fiery New Orleans entrées (just right with jazz), homemade pastas, steaks, and specialties such as Chicken Martinelli (boneless breast, braised with oysters, herb butter, and sparkling apple cider), veal and seafood.

The house dessert, Boule de Niege, is a rich, dense mound of chocolate, frosted with whipped cream. Split one with a friend, or try the equally delicious cheesecake with apple strudel topping.

Dee Felice Café, 529 Main Street, Covington, is open 7 days a week. Lunch, Monday through Friday, is 11 a.m. to 3 p.m.; dinner is 5 to 10 p.m. Sunday through Tuesday, to 11 p.m. Wednesday and Thursday, and to 12:00 midnight Friday and Saturday. (606)261-2365. There is jazz every night, dress is casual, and all beverages are served, including Sunday; reservations are requested, especially on weekends. AE,DC,MC,V. ($$)

DEE FELICE CAFÉ MUSSELS GINO

1 ounce butter
A "tad" of garlic
A "tad" of shallots
14 mussels, in the shell
3 Tablespoons
  chopped parsley
Salt and pepper to taste
2/3 cup good white
  dry wine
Lemon wedge for garnish

In saucepan, heat butter with garlic and shallots until hot. Add mussels, parsley, salt and pepper. Sprinkle with wine, cover, and steam until done, about four or five minutes. Serve opened mussels in a ring with a lemon wedge. Serves 1.

DUDLEY'S RESTAURANT

Lexington City School No. 3, known as The Dudley School, was constructed in 1881 on the site of a residence which had housed the school since its creation in 1851. It was named for Dr. Benjamin Winslow Dudley, a Lexington surgeon, chairman of anatomy and surgery departments at Transylvania University Medical School.

The two-story, late Richardsonian brick structure remained a school until 1932. One early instructor was Mary Desha, a founder of the Daughters of the American Revolution.

The building housed various government offices during depression and war years, but was vacant seven years before restoration. With the South Hill Historic District, it was placed on the National Register in 1978, and in 1980, it became a mall of specialty shops and Dudley's Restaurant.

Owners Deborah Long and John Shea carefully adapted available space; entered from the wide hallway that echoes with footsteps of generations of school children, Dudley's seems always to have been a restaurant. Restful shades of plum and green are set off by natural wood and plants; the ex-classroom bar is cozy, and the dining room (former Principal's office) is lighted by tall windows and graced with candles and flowers. In warm weather, diners linger on the patio under umbrellas and a huge sycamore tree.

Food at Dudley's receives extra attention: everything is fresh and cooked to order, accommodating those on special diets. Local foods are treated in non-traditional ways, with daily appetizer, soup, fish and seafood specials, and a menu of "regulars," and rich, varied desserts. Hot muffins are different each day, often combining many flavoring ingredients, and are always superb.

Dudley's Restaurant, 380 South Mill Street, Lexington, is open 7 days a week. Lunch is 11:30 a.m. to 2:30 p.m., and dinner is 5:30 to 10 p.m. weekdays, until 11 p.m. Friday and Saturday. Lighter fare is available from 2:30 p.m. to 5:30 p.m. in the bar. (606)252-1010. Dress is casual, all legal beverages are served, and reservations are always a good idea, essential on weekends. AE,MC,V. ($$)

DUDLEY'S POPPY SEED MUFFINS

2 cups flour	1 1/4 cups milk
1/4 cup sugar	1 egg
Pinch of salt	1/4 cup dark corn syrup
2 heaping teaspoons baking powder	1/4 cup melted butter
	2 Tablespoons poppy seed

Mix all ingredients in order, being careful not to over-mix. Spoon into greased muffin tins, and bake at 350 degrees 15 to 20 minutes in regular oven, about 12 minutes in convection oven. To vary flavor, substitute 1/4 cup raisins, nuts, or drained crushed pineapple for poppy seed, or use 1 teaspoon cinnamon, ginger, or other spice, or a combination. Brown sugar may be substituted for granulated, or honey for corn syrup. Yields 12 large muffins.

BEAUMONT INN

The oldest permanent settlement west of the Alleghenies, Harrodsburg was founded in June, 1774. James Harrod and 30 companions paddled down the Monongahela and Ohio Rivers and up the Kentucky River, then trekked overland to Big Spring, where they built a fort.

Women and children arrived in the fall of 1775, bringing civilization to the wilderness, and the outpost rapidly grew into a gracious town, known for its culture and social life.

Among the many handsome Greek Revival structures remaining in Harrodsburg is white-columned Beaumont Inn, built in the 1840s as a boarding school. It continued in successful operation until 1914, when its president and owner died. In 1918, Annie Bell Goddard, a graduate and former dean, opened Beaumont Inn, converting the college's spacious rooms into a country inn of great distinction.

Placed on the National Register of Historic Places in 1980, it is now operated by the third and fourth generations of her family.

Beaumont Inn is the focal point of 30 wooded acres; guests are welcomed in a front hall filled with memorabilia of General

Robert E. Lee, and may meet friends in a double parlor furnished with period antiques. Large dining rooms in gold, green, and pumpkin colors are settings for arrangements of fruits, vegetables, and flowers, depending upon the season, but the famous traditional Kentucky food is the stellar attraction.

Fried "yellow-legged" chicken and carefully aged country ham top a menu of Southern favorites, and these, plus a daily special entrée, are accompanied by appetizer, salad, vegetables (including their renowned corn pudding), and homemade biscuits. Among old-fashioned desserts are their famous Robert E. Lee and Chocolate Sherry cakes, fruits in meringues and cobblers, Fig Pudding, and Huguenot Torte.

Beaumont Inn, 638 Beaumont Drive, Harrodsburg, is open from mid-March until mid-December. Breakfast is served only to overnight guests, and lunch seatings are at 12:00 noon and 1:15 p.m., Tuesday through Saturday, 12:00 noon and 1:30 p.m. Sunday. Dinner seatings are 6 and 7:30 p.m., Monday through Saturday, and 6 p.m. only on Sunday. (606)734-3381. Dress is casual (shorts not allowed in evenings) and reservations are strongly advised. There are 33 overnight units. AE,MC,V. ($$)

BEAUMONT INN
CARROT OR ASPARAGUS SOUFFLÉ*

1 cup cooked,	1 1/4 cups milk
ground carrots	1 Tablespoon sugar
OR 1 cup	1/2 teaspoon salt
asparagus pieces	1 Tablespoon
1 Tablespoon flour	melted butter
1 egg, beaten	

Mix carrots (or asparagus) with flour. Mix egg and milk, and combine the two mixtures. Add sugar, salt, and butter and stir well. Pour into buttered casserole, and bake at 375 degrees, stirring occasionally until mixture begins to thicken. Bake until firm but not dry.

*From BEAUMONT INN SPECIAL RECIPES. Harrodsburg, Kentucky. Used by permission.

THE SHAKER VILLAGE OF PLEASANT HILL

I n this charming community, twenty-eight 19th-century buildings have been restored on 2600 acres of beautiful rolling farmland, the largest and most complete of any Shaker colony still in existence.

A National Historic Landmark from boundary to boundary since 1972, "Shakertown" was one of 18 Shaker communities founded during the late 18th and early 19th centuries.

The United Society of Believers in Christ's Second Appearing were known as "Shakers" due to the dance-like form of their religious services. Celibate, industrious individuals from many backgrounds lived apart from "the world" in an environment of sexual and racial equality, and dedicated their lives to hard work and superior craftsmanship. The Pleasant Hill colony endured a little over a hundred years, closing in 1910, and the last Kentucky Shaker died in 1923. Evidences of their work remain at Pleasant Hill today in original Shaker furniture and tools, and their simple, very Southern adaptation of Georgian-Federal architecture.

In the restored buildings, interpreters in Shaker dress explain the strange, productive lives of the Shakers, and demonstrate Shaker crafts. During Shaker Heritage Weekends each September, additional programs of music, dance, cooking, and crafts are scheduled.

Visitors have always been welcomed to the three-story brick Trustees' House, where electric candles gleam in cherry sconces, simple muslin curtains tall windows, and twin staircases spiral upward in simple beauty. In the dining rooms, regional Kentucky foods, seasonal favorites, and Shaker specialties are served at the table by waitresses in Shaker dress, with no limit to "helpings" of the delicious fresh vegetables.

No one leaves Shakertown hungry; full though you may be, you are cautioned to "Shaker your plate," and like Pleasant Hill's original residents, leave nothing to waste.

The Shaker Village of Pleasant Hill is on US 68, 25 miles southwest of Lexington and 7 miles northeast of Harrodsburg. (606)734-5411. Three meals a day are served in seatings; reservations are strongly advised. Dress is casual, and there is a strict no-tipping policy. Lodging is available in 15 original buildings. No charge cards are accepted. ($$)

PLEASANT HILL POPCORN SOUP*

2 1/2 cups fresh corn, cut off cob and chopped
1 cup milk
3 Tablespoons butter
1/2 medium onion, chopped

3 Tablespoons flour
1 1/2 teaspoons salt
Dash of pepper
2 1/2 cups milk
1/2 cup half and half
Popcorn

Cook corn in 1 cup milk until tender. Melt butter and sauté onion until soft. Stir in flour, salt, and pepper, then additional milk, half and half, and cooked corn. Cook until thickened. Sprinkle top of soup with popcorn before serving. Serves 4.

*From WE MAKE YOU KINDLY WELCOME by Elizabeth C. Kremer. Harrodsburg, Kentucky. Copyright 1970. Used by permission.

SCIENCE HILL INN

$\mathbf{W}$hen Julia Ann Tevis moved to Shelbyville with her Methodist clergyman husband in 1824, she opened Science Hill Female Academy, a serious school for girls. It was not expected to succeed—young ladies had little need of "boys' subjects." Nevertheless, 20 students enrolled, and the school expanded to include a total of 78 rooms surrounding a courtyard, which was enclosed in 1848.

By that time, there were more than 200 pupils, and John Tevis had given up the ministry to become spiritual head of the school. Science Hill continued in operation until 1939 with only one change in ownership, maintaining an outstanding reputation for education.

The building was used for a time as a residential inn, and in 1947, Mark Scearce opened Wakefield-Scearce Galleries in the chapel, showing antiques, silver, and decorative accessories. In 1960, he bought the entire structure, and today the internationally known gallery shares the former school with specialty shops and a restaurant, Science Hill Inn. It was placed on the National Register in 1975.

Science Hill Inn, operated since 1978 by Terry and Donna

Gill, who were joined by their daughter Ellen in 1988, presents updated traditional Kentucky fare in the high-ceilinged Georgian dining room where good food has been served for 150 years.

Tall windows on two sides overlook shady old gardens, and fresh flowers and white linens gleam in the sunlight. Here you'll find Kentucky Bibb lettuce salad (with artichoke hearts, turkey, cheese, and country ham), or Kentucky trout, chicken, steaks, country ham, special salads and elegant sandwiches, plus a choice of rich homemade desserts.

The Sunday buffet, served on silver from the Wakefield-Scearce vault, always offers fried chicken, country ham, and barbecued brisket of beef with corn pudding and country-style green beans, and may include zucchini casserole, cauliflower with mustard mayonnaise, tomato pudding, cucumber mousse, and wild rice salad, with buttermilk biscuits and hot water corn bread. This is Kentucky hospitality at its best, and there's still dessert....

Science Hill Inn, 525 Washington Street, Shelbyville, is open for lunch Tuesday through Saturday, 2:30 p.m. Sunday buffet is 11:30 a.m. to 2:30 p.m. (502)633-2825. Dress is casual, all legal beverages are served, and reservations are suggested, especially during November and December. AE,MC,V. ($$)

SCIENCE HILL INN CUCUMBER MOUSSE*

2 Tablespoons plain gelatin	1 1/2 cups sour cream
1 medium cucumber	2 teaspoons salt
2 cups mayonnaise	2 Tablespoons dill weed
	2 Tablespoons lemon juice

In a saucepan, sprinkle gelatin over 1/2 cup water and set aside. Peel, seed, and shred cucumber and place in mixing bowl. Add next five ingredients and mix well. Over low heat dissolve gelatin; add to cucumber mixture. Pour into oiled 1 1/2 quart mold and chill until set.

* From DONNA GILL RECOMMENDS. Shelbyville, Kentucky. Used by permission.

TRAIN STATION RESTAURANT

Although the town of Anchorage was settled in 1783, it reached its peak a hundred years later, when residential areas were laid out according to a Frederick Law Olmstead design for a garden community.

Here, safe from the Yellow Fever and Malaria that threatened Louisville, wealthy people summered on spacious estates, while businessmen commuted from downtown on the Interurban railway.

Interurban lines utilized electric traction cars—like long distance streetcars with heavier, faster bodies—to connect towns by public transportation. The Louisville and Eastern Railroad reached Anchorage in 1901, and a charming frame station was built for passengers and freight.

Anchorage became a year-round "bedroom community" for Louisville, but competition from automobiles brought an end to interurban lines, and after trains stopped running, the little station served in several capacities, including dress shop and gift shop. It was placed on the National Register in 1980, and became a restaurant in 1987.

Leonard Lusky, owner, increased the size of the building so

skillfully that its original dimensions are hard to detect; he won the 1988 Historical Preservation Award for best commercial renovation in the county. This attention to detail is apparent in the food served in the Train Station, as well, with cosmopolitan treatments of highest quality ingredients.

Surrounded with art works, overlooking gardens and a lush "tropical deck" used for dining when weather permits, guests relax and enjoy Shrimp Cortez (stuffed with Monterey Jack, wrapped in bacon in a spicy barbecue sauce) or Newmarket Filet of Certified Angus beef, served with Maderia and Béarnaise sauces.

Desserts are no less special; a summer favorite is Triple Berry Shortcake with Chantilly Crème, White Chocolate Mousse Torte is always special, but beyond description is something called Chocolate Inferno.

The Train Station Restaurant, 1500 Evergreen Road, Anchorage, is about 1 mile north of US 60, and is open Wednesday through Monday, 5 p.m. until 12:00 midnight. (502)245-7121. All legal beverages are served, dress is "tennis to tux," and reservations are suggested on weekends. AE,CB,DC,MC,V. ($$)

TRAIN STATION SHRIMP AND CRAB FRITTERS

2 Tablespoons butter	1 pound crab meat
2 ribs celery,	1 cup flour
finely chopped	4 eggs
1/2 medium onion,	1 Tablespoon
finely chopped	baking powder
1 pound shrimp,	Salt and pepper
peeled and deveined	Béarnaise Sauce*

In large skillet, melt butter; add celery and onion and sauté until onion is transparent. Add remaining ingredients and stir until blended, adding more flour if mixture appears too thin—it should be thick enough to form a ball. Use teaspoon to scoop golfball-sized fritters; deep fry in 350 degree oil until golden. Serve with Béarnaise Sauce. Yields 20 to 25 fritters.

*Béarnaise Sauce may be found in any good standard cookbook.

THE WHISTLE STOP RESTAURANT

In the quaint country village of Glendale, white houses starched with gingerbread sprawl in shady yards, neighbors wave as they go about their business, and the only disturbers of the peace are passing trains.

The station is gone now; trains are fewer and no longer stop, but the track still runs through town, and the flavor of the railroad years has been preserved in The Whistle Stop restaurant.

In 1974, James and Idell Sego rebuilt part of his trackside hardware store into a restaurant, incorporating ticket windows and other train station elements. A tumble-down log cabin was rebuilt next to the restaurant as a cozy waiting room with a gift shop in the loft.

Expansion of The Whistle Stop eventually absorbed the entire building, with dining areas made to look like separate small buildings within the large one. One room, long and narrow as a train dining car, has booths on each side; another has a gabled roof overhead, a third is a country kitchen, complete with dry sink and pump, wood stove, and cupboards cluttered with vintage implements.

All the country charm isn't in the decor, however. Idell's imagination produces nostalgic American food with up-to-date taste.

"Trainman Specials" include creamed chicken on corn bread, and baked pork chops with potatoes and cream sauce; dinner specials might be pan-fried trout, salmon croquettes or stuffed pork chops, served with fresh country vegetables, salad, and homemade bread. Puffy hot rolls and fried corn bread are outstanding, and homemade soups and old-fashioned desserts can't be beat. Sugar Cream Pie (meltingly sweet, with cinnamon) and other pies and fruit cobblers have flaky light crusts; if you call ahead, you can take one home. Better yet, take two!

The Whistle Stop Restaurant, Main Street, Glendale, is open Tuesday through Saturday, 11 a.m. to 9 p.m., with a limited menu from 2 to 5 p.m. Dress is casual, and no reservations or credit cards are accepted; personal checks accepted. The Iron Horse Dining Room on the second floor offers a more elaborate menu from 4:30 to 9 p.m.; reservations are accepted. (502)369-8586. ($$)

WHISTLE STOP KENTUCKY BIBB LETTUCE WITH HOT BACON DRESSING

Medium bowl of Bibb
  or leaf lettuce
3 or 4 fresh green onions
  with tops, chopped
4 Tablespoons
  bacon drippings

2 Tablespoons
  white vinegar
1 teaspoon sugar
Salt and pepper
4 slices crisp bacon,
  crumbled

Wash and drain lettuce and tear into bite-sized pieces. Place in bowl and toss with onions. Set aside. In iron skillet, heat bacon drippings, vinegar, sugar, salt and pepper just to boiling. Pour over lettuce, and toss lightly. Top with crumbled bacon. Serves 4 to 6.

BARTHOLOMEW'S

In 1796, North Carolinian Bartholomew Wood built a log cabin at The Rock Spring, a landmark near the crossing of the Russellville trail and the Little River, in western Kentucky.

A new county was established, named for Patrick Henry's brother-in-law, Colonel William Christian, a Revolutionary War hero killed by Indians during settlement of Louisville. Bartholomew Wood donated five acres of land to the town originally named Elizabeth, but renamed for General Samuel Hopkins in 1804.

Wood is commemorated by two monuments: a statue in Hopkinsville's pioneer cemetery, and a restaurant on the site of his original cabin.

Bartholomew's occupies a brick, terra cotta and stone Romanesque structure built in 1894 as The Racket Store, selling buggies and general merchandise. As part of the Christian County Multiple Resource area, it was placed on the National Register in 1979.

In 1982, the lower portion was adapted as the dining room,

and the mezzanine, left from a 1920s remodeling, as the bar; upper floors are used for offices and a banquet room. The open, airy restaurant is filled with plants, light, and photographs of Hopkinsville's past, including a picture of Wood's son, and a copy of the original deed to the property.

Bartholomew's approach to food is clever and caring, featuring fresh ingredients and unusual combinations. Ground chuck burgers with various toppings are on egg batter buns with sharp Cheddar cheese; French fries are cut from fresh potatoes; entrées are interestingly prepared and generously served; and homemade desserts and dessert drinks are rich and innovative. Don't miss the Strawberry Shortcake drink!

Bartholomew's, 914 South Main Street, Hopkinsville, is on the corner of 10th Street. Lunch, Monday through Friday, is 11 a.m. to 2:30 p.m.; dinner, Monday through Thursday, is 5 to 9:30 p.m., Friday until 11 p.m. Saturday hours are 11 a.m. to 11 p.m. (502)886-5768. Dress is informal, all beverages are served, and reservations are not accepted; call ahead for preferred seating. AE,MC,V. ($$)

BARTHOLOMEW'S LOADED POTATO SOUP

2 cups coarsely
  chopped celery
2 cups coarsely
  chopped white onion
2 cups 1" sliced carrots
3/4 teaspoon white pepper

2 quarts chicken stock
2 cups 1 1/2" potato cubes
1 cup whipping cream
1/2 cup flour, blended with
  2 Tablespoons butter

In large pan, place vegetables, pepper, and stock. Boil until vegetables are tender; add potato cubes and cream; simmer 15 or 20 minutes. Add some of the flour/butter mixture to thicken; all may not be needed. Simmer to cook flour. Correct seasonings and add salt if necessary. Serves 10 to 12.

THE NINTH STREET HOUSE

In 1795, for service during the Revolution, General George Rogers Clark was awarded substantial acreage in what is now Western Kentucky. He willed a tract at the confluence of the Ohio and Tennessee rivers to his brother General William Clark, noted for his exploration of the West with Meriwether Lewis. Clark renamed the existing village of Pekin for friendly Indian Chief Paduke. Only 50 miles from the Mississippi, Paducah's early success was tied to river traffic; it grew rapidly as an industrial and commercial center.

A great-nephew of the Clarks, George Wallace, built a handsome Queen Anne-style winter home in Paducah's "Lower Town" in 1886. Threatened with demolition, it was rescued by present owners Curtis and Norma Grace to became a restaurant in 1974, spearheading restoration in a 30-block area. The Lower Town Historic District was placed on The National Register in 1982.

The Ninth Street House, restored to its original glory, has the dark woodwork, stained and beveled glass, and elegance of the Victorian era, enhanced by antiques of the period, including an 1865 Steinway played on week-end nights. Beneath the decorative mantels in each dining room, fires are lighted on c evenings, adding to the feeling of candlelit intimacy.

"Classic Southern Cooking" at The Ninth Street House always offers fresh seafood, prime rib, and lamb, plus nightly specials, vegetables cooked to order, and homemade breads, dressings, and ice creams. Curtis' marvelous desserts vary, but frequently feature crisp pastry, fresh fruit, and gobs of whipped cream.

Luncheon fare includes homemade soups, unusual sandwiches, and popular curry-scented California Chicken Salad. The iced tea, a house secret, has been called "the best in the world!"

The Ninth Street House, 323 Ninth Street, Paducah, is open Tuesday through Saturday. Lunch is 11 a.m. to 2 p.m., and dinner is 6 to 8:30 p.m., weeknights, until 9 p.m. Friday and Saturday. (502)442-9019. Dress is informal, and reservations are suggested; all legal beverages are served. DC,MC,V. ($$)

NINTH STREET HOUSE PECAN CRISPIES

1 cup butter or margarine
1/2 cup sugar
1 teaspoon vanilla

1/2 cup crushed
 potato chips
1/2 cup chopped pecans
2 cups sifted flour

Cream butter, sugar and vanilla. Add crushed potato chips and pecans. Stir in flour. Roll into small balls. Place on ungreased cookie sheet and press ball flat with bottom of tumbler dipped in sugar. Bake at 350 degrees for 16 to 18 minutes or until lightly browned. Yields approximately 3 dozen cookies.

*From COOK TALK WITH CURTIS GRACE, Copyright 1989 Curtis Grace, Kuttawa, Kentucky. Used by permission.

LOUISIANA

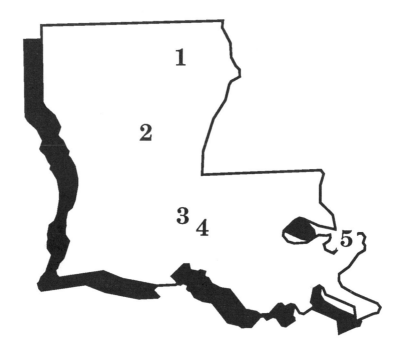

1. MONROE
   Chef Hans' Restaurant
2. ALEXANDRIA
   Hotel Bentley
3. LAFAYETTE
   Café Vermilionville
4. BROUSSARD
   Vive La Différence
5. NEW ORLEANS
   Christian's
   Kolb's
   Commander's Palace

CHEF HANS' RESTAURANT

Hernando de Soto crossed the Ouachita River in 1542 on his westward search for gold. Although the area was mapped by the French in 1700, and a trading post was established 20 years later, there was no permanent European settlement until after the French and Indian Wars when Louisiana was ceded to Spain.

Jean Baptiste Filhiol, commandant of the Poste des Washitas, established a town on the present site of Monroe in 1785, and Fort Miro was erected in 1790.

In 1819, the Steamboat *James Monroe* reached the settlement, providing transportation for cotton crops and ushering in prosperity. The town, re-named to honor the boat and the President, became the trading center of Northeast Louisiana.

In the early 20th century, Monroe's North Side became a residential suburb, considered to be 'way out in the country. A Dr. Marx built a comfortable frame bungalow at the corner of 3rd and Bres, with a wide porch and generously sized rooms. In 1981, it was chosen by Chef Hans Korrodi, a Swiss with an extensive European and American background, to become his restaurant. Painted pink with white trim, its inviting exterior is echoed inside with shades of peach, maroon, and dark green.

Chef Hans combines his Continental experience with Louisiana's fresh foods and traditional flavors to create a very special cuisine; he was a pioneer in the use of soft shell crawfish (his are fried in beer batter, served en brochette with a spicy brown sauce) and has developed his own line of packaged mixes and spice blends.

Everything here is fresh, "Or we don't have it!" Veal and steaks are hand-cut, and European favorites (Wienerschnitzel, Châteaubriand) join Blackened Redfish, Gumbo, and Alligator Soup for as wide a variety as you'll find. Desserts range from cheesecakes to bread pudding to Bananas Foster—from Chef Hans' own mix you can take home.

Chef Hans' Restaurant, 819 North 3rd Street, Monroe, is open for lunch Tuesday through Friday, 11:30 a.m. to 2 p.m. Dinner, Tuesday through Saturday, is 6 to 9 p.m. (318)322-6907. All legal beverages are served, dress is casual or dressy, and reservations are requested. The restaurant is closed the first week in January and the last week in September. AE,MC,V. ($$$)

CHEF HANS' VEAL NEW ORLEANS

24 ounces veal,
  thinly sliced
1 Tablespoon flour
2 Tablespoons butter
  or margarine
4 artichoke hearts,
  quartered
1/4 pound
  sliced mushrooms
2 Tablespoons
  chopped green onion

1 Tablespoon
  chopped parsley
1 ounce white wine
1/4 cup
  half and half cream
Cayenne pepper
Coarse ground
  black pepper
Salt

Dredge veal in flour. Melt butter in hot skillet, add veal, stir and brown lightly. Add next 2 ingredients, simmer 1 minute, reduce heat to low, then add next 3 ingredients, and mix well. Remove from heat, add cream, and season to taste. Do not cook after adding cream or ingredients will separate. Serves 4.

HOTEL BENTLEY

Rapids in the Red River caused navigation problems, and a portage was required for passage when water was low. Nearby, a group of Indians settled when their land was ceded to the British in 1763. French, Spanish, Acadians, and Anglo-Saxons arrived, with African slaves, and from this base a multi-cultural town grew, formally laid out in 1810 and named for the daughter of a wealthy landowner.

Supported by steamboat traffic, Alexandria and its sister-city, Pineville, became a center for shipping and trade, but both were burned by retreating Federal troops after the Battle of Mansfield in 1864.

After Reconstruction—during which troops under General George Custer mutinied here—the towns were rebuilt. The growing lumber industry attracted Joseph Bentley, a Pennsylvanian, who built Hotel Bentley in 1908. According to legend, he did so when prohibited from keeping his dog in another hotel.

The handsome Neoclassical building was remodeled and enlarged in 1937, incorporating elements of Art Deco style; contractor Simon Tudor took the marble fish pool, discarded from the lobby, to his own garden.

A popular stopover for politicians and entertainers, the Bentley also housed family and commanders of the many military personnel stationed nearby during World War II.

As downtown waned, the Bentley was sold and finally stood empty, but it was placed on the National Register in 1979. In 1983 it was purchased by the Tudor family, who restored it to its earlier elegance, and returned the fish pool to the lobby.

In the hotel's former coffee shop, now the Bentley Room, Chef Jacques Fox provides a generous weekday lunch buffet that includes regional favorites such as Crawfish Pie, and Sausage and Beans with Cornbread. Dinner is drawn from classic French cuisine, again with regional touches (superb gumbo) and fresh local seafoods. Popular are Seafood Pasta, veal dishes, and charbroiled beef and seafoods. The dessert cart includes cheesecakes, pecan pie, carrot cake, and rich, dark Chocolate Bourbon Cake.

The Bentley Room of the Hotel Bentley, 200 De Soto Street, Alexandria, is open 7 days a week. Breakfast is 6:30 to 11 a.m.; lunch and Sunday brunch are 11 a.m. to 2 p.m.; and dinner is 6 to 10 p.m., Sunday to 9 p.m. (318)448-9600. All legal beverages are served, there is no dress code, and reservations are recommended. There are 315 overnight rooms. AE,CB,DS,MC,V. ($$$)

HOTEL BENTLEY
GRENADINE DE VEAU BENTLEY

4 ounces (3 slices)   2 ounces jumbo lump
 baby veal   crab meat
Seasoned flour   2 ounces crawfish tails
Butter and oil for sautéing   Béarnaise Sauce*

Pound veal slices; dredge in seasoned flour and sauté in butter and oil. In another pan, heat crab meat and crawfish in butter. Arrange veal slices on plate, top with seafood, and nap with Béarnaise Sauce. Serves 1.

*Béarnaise Sauce may be found in any good standard cookbook.

CAFÉ VERMILIONVILLE

Acadians, Nova Scotian French emigrants expelled from Canada in the 1750s, settled in the bayous and prairies of south-central Louisiana. There they engaged in beef and dairy farming; several established large plantations, and one wealthy plantation owner, Jean Mouton, donated land for the courthouse in the village of Vermilionville, named for the rust-colored water of a nearby bayou. The name was changed to Lafayette in 1884.

An inn that catered to early travelers came into the possession of Henry Louis Monnier, a Swiss, about 1853, but is believed to have existed before 1800. After housing Federal troops during the War Between the States, it was purchased by M. E. Girard in 1882, and operated as a nursery by his descendants, and by Maurice Heymann, developer of the Oil Center, after its purchase in 1939.

Rescued from proposed demolition by Horace Rickey, it was a dwelling for many years, during which the hexagonal "garçonniere" and rooms to the rear were added, and the original galleried structure restored. It was placed on the National Register in 1983, and today is Café Vermilionville, serving outstanding Louisiana French cuisine.

Owner-Chef Ken Veron uses indigenous products—shell-fish, fish, lots of crawfish—that are fresh every day; if not up to his exacting standards, they are not served. Simply prepared by sautéing and grilling, his foods achieve their flavor from home-grown herbs and unusual combinations: Kahlúa Grilled Shrimp, Swordfish Grand Marnier, and veal topped with crawfish in a Nantua sauce.

Desserts, too, are special. Bread pudding here has a lemon glaze, there's homemade ice cream, Chocolate Sin, and Angel's Cream—a chilled caramel parfait covered with whipped cream.

Café Vermilionville, 1304 West Pinhook Road, Lafayette, is open 7 days a week. Lunch, Monday through Friday, is 11 a.m. to 2 p.m.; dinner, Monday through Saturday, is 5:30 to 10 p.m.; Sunday Champagne Jazz Brunch is 10:30 a.m. to 2 p.m. (318)237-0100. All legal beverages are served, most men wear coat and tie, and reservations are recommended, especially during Mardi Gras and other festivals in spring and fall. AE,MC,V. ($$$)

CAFÉ VERMILIONVILLE CRAWFISH CAPELLINI

1 cup diced onion
1/2 cup diced green pepper
1/2 cup diced
  red bell pepper
1 teaspoon fennel seeds
1/2 pound butter
1 pound crawfish tails
1 Tablespoon
  fresh chopped basil

1 teaspoon seasoned salt
1 teaspoon Trappey's
  hot sauce or Tabasco
2 cups heavy cream
1 pound angel hair pasta,
  cooked
1 cup fresh grated
Parmesan cheese

In large sauté pan, sauté first 4 ingredients in butter about 5 minutes. Add next 5 ingredients and reduce until slightly thickened; add pasta and cheese and cook to desired consistency. Thin with additional cream, if necessary, and sprinkle with additional cheese. Serves 6.

VIVE LA DIFFÉRENCE

Among the earliest Acadian settlers was Joseph Broussard, Captain of Militia and Commandant of Acadians in 1765. Known as "Beausoleil" (sunshine) for his smile, he was a founder of the large family for which the town was named. Its early economy was based on sugar mills, but as oil became more important, it became a "bedroom community" for Lafayette.

In 1908, Edmond Comeaux and his wife Cecile Lena St. Julien built a dramatic Queen Anne-style house with an onion-domed turret, semi-octagonal bays on each side, double front gables, and a balconied dormer. It became a restaurant in 1981, and was placed on the National Register in 1983.

The interior, charmingly decorated in shades of cream, rose, and maroon, provides an elegant, welcoming atmosphere. Here, Chef Ken Koval presents contemporary American/Continental cuisine with Louisiana accents. Local products are enhanced by rich natural stocks, and everything is made on the premises—breads, sauces, desserts, dressings and "Soups of Substance."

Lunch might be Crawfish au Gratin, Broiled Filet of Catfish, or Breast of Chicken Marsala, with appetizer included; four-course dinners offer numerous appetizer choices, plus salad and dessert, with price determined by entrée. Appealing are Roast Loin of Lamb with Spinach, Baked Duckling with Black Bean Sauce, Louisiana Crawfish au Gratin, and Filet of Flounder stuffed with crawfish.

Desserts are outstanding: Lemon Mousse, Chocolate Cheese Cake, homemade ice creams, and often cheese-stuffed peaches or pears topped with berry sauces.

Vive La Différence, 101 East 2nd Street, Broussard, is open for a fixed-price, 2-course lunch 11:30 a.m. to 2 p.m. Tuesday through Friday and Sunday; for a fixed-price, 4-course dinner 5:30 to 10 p.m. Tuesday through Sunday. (318)837-2937. Broussard is 12 miles south of Lafayette on LA 182, or exit B off US 90. All legal beverages are served, dress is casual, and reservations are accepted, requested for parties of 6 or more. AE,DC,MC,V. ($$$)

VIVE LA DIFFÉRENCE
EGGPLANT AND CRAB MEDALLION

2 ounces butter
2 ounces onion,
  diced small
1 ounce celery, diced
1/2 ounce carrot, diced
5 ounces lump crab meat
1 Tablespoon flour

2 ounces heavy cream
1 Tablespoon
  chopped parsley
Salt and pepper
1 medium eggplant
2 eggs, beaten
Flour and bread crumbs

Melt butter and sauté next 3 ingredients until onions are transparent. Add crab and cook 1 minute. Sprinkle with flour and mix gently, then add cream and parsley, and season to taste. Refrigerate. Cut 1/4 inch off each end of eggplant, peel, and cut 6 1/2-inch slices from bottom end. Make 3 eggplant sandwiches with crab filling. Sprinkle with water, salt, and pepper. Dredge eggplant in flour, dip in beaten egg, then dredge in bread crumbs. Fry in deep fat at 350 degrees and serve with any sauce. Smaller eggplant slices may be used for hors d'oeuvres.

CHRISTIAN'S

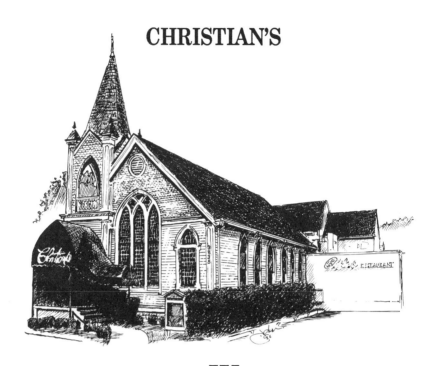

With its French and Spanish heritage, New Orleans has always been predominantly Catholic; indeed, there were early laws prohibiting public practice of any other religion. After the Louisiana Purchase, freedom of worship was proclaimed, and by mid-19th century, there were 4 Episcopalian, 13 Methodist, 6 Presbyterian, 3 Jewish, and 4 Lutheran congregations in New Orleans.

In 1914, in front of 1904 classrooms, a mid-city Lutheran church was built, combining Gothic Revival and Queen Anne styles: pointed-arch windows, patterned shingles, and an offset bell tower. Sold in 1950 to another church, in 1977, it became the new location of Christian's, Chris Ansel's well-known restaurant.

Classrooms, raised and tied to the main building, became kitchens; in the former church, false ceilings were removed, revealing original dark beams now set off by cream walls. The open interior is inviting, a relaxed setting for excellent food.

Ansel, of the famed Galatoire family, with partner Henry Bergeron and Chef Roland Huet, favors an innovative New Orleans cuisine. French influences are apparent, Créole traditions are followed in some dishes, but Christian's has its own flavor.

Everything here is homemade—breads, desserts, rich ice creams and fruit ices—prepared with attention to detail and an eye to health. Fresh seafood accounts for 75 per cent of dinners, but Duck Blackberry Vinegar, Smoked Soft Shelled Crab, and Filet Mignon stuffed and garnished with oysters are a few other popular entrées. The entirely à la carte menu gives diners a chance to create their own meal, and their own wonderful memories.

Christian's, 3835 Iberville Street, New Orleans, is open for dinner Monday through Saturday, 5:30 to 10 p.m. (504)482-4924. All legal beverages are served, proper attire is required (coat and tie preferred), and reservations are recommended, especially on weekends. The restaurant is closed 4 days at Mardi Gras. AE,CB,DC,MC,V. ($$)

CHRISTIAN'S BOUILLABAISSE

1/3 cup olive oil	6 cups fish stock
1 onion, finely sliced	16 shrimp, peeled
3 cloves garlic, chopped	12 oysters
1/2 bay leaf	1/4 pound crab meat
1/4 teaspoon thyme	8 fish filets
1/8 teaspoon	(trout, redfish, etc.)
powdered anise	1/4 teaspoon
1 tomato, peeled,	powdered saffron
seeded, and crushed	Garlic bread rounds*
1/2 cup white wine	Rouille*

In very large skillet, heat oil and sauté onion until transparent. Add next 7 ingredients and simmer uncovered about 15 minutes, or until onions are tender. Add seafood and simmer just until filets are tender; do not overcook. Add saffron and serve immediately, very hot. Pass bread and rouille. Serves 4 to 6.

For garlic bread rounds: cut 1/4" slices of French bread (about 6 per person), baste with olive oil and finely chopped garlic, and toast until light brown.

*For rouille: Make a mayonnaise using 3 egg yolks (room temperature) and 2 cups olive oil; add 1 heaping teaspoon garlic and 3/4 teaspoon cayenne pepper.

KOLB'S

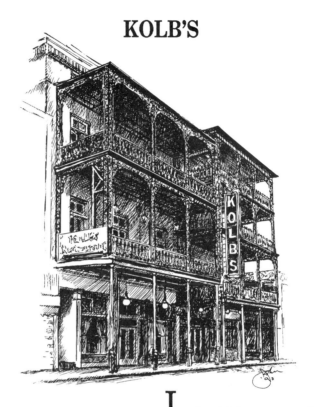

In the 19th century, New Orleans' French residents lived in the Vieux Carré, "Americans" and Irish in Faubourg St. Mary. Germans who settled in Faubourg Marigny in the 1840's accounted for a sixth of the city's population by 1860. The factions could not agree, and for 17 years the city had three separate governments.

During this period, the two buildings which house Kolb's (pronounced cobs) Restaurant were erected; No. 125 was built before 1844, occupied by a short-lived museum, followed by the Louisiana Jockey Club, and No. 119 existed before 1853. Their lacy galleries appear in a War Between the States-era illustration.

Valentine Merz operated a saloon here in 1886, when a ceiling fan system used at both the 1884 World's Industrial and Cotton Centennial Exposition, and the North, Central, and South American Exposition of 1885-86 was installed. Remarkable in its longevity, it was operated by water power until electricity came to this part of the city, and is believed to be the oldest working fan system in the United States.

Conrad Kolb, a bartender for Merz, succeeded as owner, installing millwork from Germany and focussing on German beer and food. He was an enterprising and successful businessman, and much of the restaurant's quaint charm can be attributed to him.

On the outskirts of notorious "Storyville," Kolb's advertised a respectable "Ladies' Restaurant" adjacent to the main tavern downstairs, but provided less refined entertainment upstairs.

Still maintaining its German flavor, Kolb's offers unique hybrid items—Schnitzel Ponchartrain, with shrimp, crab meat and fresh vegetables in a wine-butter sauce, and Kolb's Schnitzel, topped with lump crab meat in sherry and shallots—as well as traditional Continental specialties and local seafoods. Soups, salads, and "Overstuffed Sandwiches" enhance lunch, and desserts include Apple Strudel Cheesecake and Eva's Kiss Cake—a sandwich of homemade poundcake and ice cream, dripping with chocolate syrup.

Kolb's, 125 St. Charles Avenue, New Orleans, is open 7 days a week. (504)522-8278. Lunch is 11 a.m. to 2:30 p.m. Monday through Saturday; dinner 5:30 to 10 p.m., nightly. All legal beverages (including many German beers and wines) are served; dress is casual, although most men wear coat and tie at lunch; and reservations are accepted, mandatory for Oktoberfest and Mardi Gras. AE,CB,DC,MC,V. ($$$)

KOLB'S BARBECUED SHRIMP

2 dozen jumbo shrimp, heads on
1/2 pound butter

1/4 cup ground black pepper
3/4 cup water

Place all ingredients in large skillet and sauté 10 to 12 minutes, basting occasionally. Kolb's secret is: When you think you have enough pepper, add more! Serve with hard French bread for dipping and lots of paper napkins.

COMMANDER'S PALACE

Beginning in 1812, when steamboats arrived on the Mississippi, New Orleans became a major port. People from all over the world flocked to the growing city; by mid-19th century, it was the third largest in the United States.

The New Orleans French found it difficult to accept the new arrivals, and as the city (and their fortunes) grew, "Americans" established their own living and business districts.

A sugar plantation just upriver was purchased by a group of American investors in 1832, and lots were sold in what became the "Garden District." Prosperous families built luxurious homes embellished with architectural details, surrounded with trees and gardens. The Garden District was named a National Historic Landmark in 1971.

In 1880, Emile Commander built a turreted Queen Anne-style house in the Garden District and opened a restaurant known for fine dining. When it came on the market in 1969, the five remaining Brennan siblings decided to leave the management of famous Brennan's restaurant to nephews, and begin again. Their success has created one of the premier restaurants in the country, providing superb food and friendly, helpful service.

Brightened by fresh colors and glass walls overlooking its lovely courtyard, the exterior a cheerful turquoise with white trim, Commander's Palace looks as if it expects guests to have a grand time. And they do.

Traditional Créole favorites are taken into the 1990s as "Haute Créole," a lightened, healthier adaptation, using only fresh ingredients of the highest quality for sparkling taste. Imagine a meal of spicy Shrimp Remoulade; Rack of Lamb with Mint-Madeira Sauce, a salad of greens, mushrooms, avocado, and crab; and fluffy Créole Bread Pudding Soufflé—all without guilt!

Commander's Palace, 1403 Washington Avenue, is open 7 days a week. Lunch is 11:30 a.m. to 2 p.m., Monday through Friday; dinner is 6 to 10 p.m. every day; Jazz Brunch seatings begin at 11:30 a.m. on Saturday, 10:30 a.m. on Sunday. (504)899-8231. All legal beverages are served, jackets are required for men at dinner and brunch, reservations are recommended. AE,CB,DC,DS,MC,V. ($$$)

COMMANDER'S PALACE
CRAB MEAT & CORN BISQUE**

1/2 pound butter	1 pound fresh lump
1 cup flour	crab meat
Crab stock*	Salt and fresh
1 teaspoon crab boil	ground pepper
Kernels from 4 ears	1 1/2 cups finely
sweet corn	chopped scallions
1 1/2 cups cream	

In large pot, melt butter. Stir in flour until it sticks to pan. Add stock and crab boil. Bring to boil, stirring; simmer 15 minutes. Add corn; simmer 15 minutes more. Stir in cream, then crab. Remove from heat; let stand 15 minutes. In double boiler, reheat to serving temperature. Season, add onions and serve. Serves 8. *For crab stock: In large pot, bring to boil 2 quarts water, shells from 6 medium crabs, and 2 medium onions, quartered. Simmer until reduced to 1 quart. Strain.

**From The Commander's Palace New Orleans Cookbook, copyright 1984, by Commander's Palace, Inc. Used with permission.

MISSISSIPPI

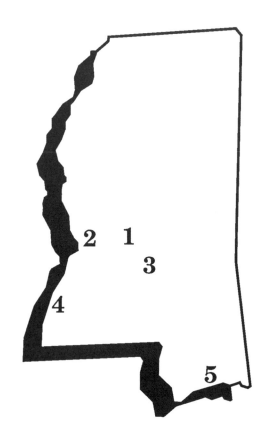

1. JACKSON
   400 East Capitol
   The Silver Platter Restaurant
2. VICKSBURG
   Old Southern Tea Room
3. MENDENHALL
   The Mendenhall Hotel
4. NATCHEZ
   The Pompous Palate
   Scrooge's Restaurant
5. BILOXI
   Mary Mahoney's Old French House
   Restaurant

400 EAST CAPITOL

L ouis Le Fleur's trading post above the Pearl River was renamed for Andrew Jackson when it became the territorial Capital. The first statehouse was replaced in 1840 by a Greek Revival Capitol, which has housed the State Historical Museum since 1961.

A block from the Old Capitol, S. J. Johnson Dry Goods opened in 1906, with one of five automatic sprinkler systems in the South. Purchased by Marks and Rothenberg in 1930, it became The Emporium department store until 1968. As part of the Smith Park Architectural District, it was placed on the National Register in 1976, and was restored in 1989 by Nick Apostle, who owns the first floor restaurant.

In high-ceilinged elegance, Classic Cuisine is beautifully presented by Apostle and co-owner Chef Grant Nooe. Fresh local ingredients—Mississippi catfish and rabbit, lamb, quail, veal, and beef—are prepared to order with vegetables chosen for each entrée.

Begin lunch with delicate cream of celery soup, followed by warm quail salad and sweet potato fries; for dinner, choose Roasted Spring Lamb in apple/lamb jus with Corn and Red

Pepper Timbale, or Grilled Stuffed Chicken with Tomato Salsa and Grilled Vegetables.

Decorative and delicious desserts include Chocolate Génoise, Raspberry Tart, Grasshopper Pie, and Chocolate Paradise: Chocolate ladyfingers with chocolate filling and Crème Anglais.

400 East Capitol, 400 East Capitol Street, Jackson, is open for lunch Monday through Friday, 11 a.m. to 2 p.m., and for dinner Monday through Saturday, 6 to 10 p.m., often later on weekends. Sunday brunch is 11 a.m. to 3 p.m. (601)355-9671. Most men wear coat and tie, all legal beverages are served, and reservations are advised, especially for parties of 6 or more. Busiest times are November and April, during the Legislature. AE,MC,V. ($$$)

400 EAST CAPITOL
OYSTER MUSHROOM TERRINE

2 1/2 cups chopped mushroom stems, reserve caps
1/2 cup chopped shallots
1 Tablespoon chopped garlic
1 Tablespoon butter
2 ounces port wine
2 ounces veal demi-glaze*
3 1/2 cups shredded Mozzarella
2 cups shredded Parmesan
3 Tablespoons chopped fresh basil
3 teaspoons chopped fresh oregano
2 Tablespoons chopped fresh parsley
Salt and pepper
3 large red bell peppers
3 large green bell peppers
3 large yellow bell peppers

In skillet over low heat, combine first 4 ingredients. Stir until shallots are translucent; add wine and demi-glaze, and reduce by half. Purée in food processor; add cheeses and herbs, purée smooth, season. Roast peppers; seed, skin, and dry. Place mushroom caps (smooth side out) on sides and bottom of 12" terrine, then layer cheese mixture and peppers, alternating colors. End with cheese and top with mushroom caps (smooth side up). Cover with buttered parchment; bake in water bath 25 minutes at 350 degrees. Refrigerate 4 hours. To serve, invert and cut 1/2" slices. Heat slices in oven 2 minutes, transfer to hot plate, and serve with tomato coulis. Serves 24 as appetizer.

*The home cook may substitute reduced, jellied chicken stock; results will be slightly different.

THE SILVER PLATTER RESTAURANT

Railroads in the South were of enormous importance during the War Between the States; inadequate at best, they were utilized to capacity. Jackson, at the intersection of two railroads, became a supply base, as well as the Confederate Capital of Mississippi.

In May, 1863, Union General U. S. Grant, on his way to the Confederate stronghold at Vicksburg, occupied and burned Jackson. After Vicksburg fell in July, Confederate forces entrenched at Jackson were besieged by General W. T. Sherman, who again burned the city. Only a few buildings were spared, giving Jackson the sad nickname of "Chimneyville".

The state penitentiary, used as a munitions factory during the war, provided the site for the "new" capitol, a massive Beaux Arts structure completed in 1903. Just a block down President Street, the Mississippi Association of Educators constructed a quaint assembly hall and textbook depository in 1925.

Larger than it seems, the one-story brick building has a tile roof with parapeted gables surmounted by stone lamps of learning. Outgrown in the 1970s, it was purchased by Maureen and Ed Watt, a couple long involved in the food industry, who wanted to open a restaurant.

Behind paneling and carpeting, they discovered thick stippled plaster walls and parquet floors. Added partitions were removed, and stained and carved woodwork were restored, resulting in a cozy, homelike restaurant which opened in 1978.

The Silver Platter's International menu brings people back for popular dishes—flaming Crown Royal Steak, duckling, and fish with sauces such as "Rebecca" (crawfish and shrimp in dark roux)—but changing soups (especially Mississippi Catfish Chowder and Gumbo) and daily specials provide interesting variety.

Desserts include Australian Pavlova (meringue cake with fruit), Créole Bread Pudding with Whiskey Sauce, and warm Amaretto Chocolate Cake mounded with whipped cream.

The Silver Platter Restaurant, 219 North President Street, Jackson, may be reached from the Pearl Street exit off I-55. It is open from 11 a.m., Monday through Friday, with continuous service, and from 5 p.m. on Sunday. (601)969-3413. All legal beverages are served, casual attire is welcomed, and reservations are accepted. AE,DC,DS,MC,V. ($$$)

SILVER PLATTER
MAGNOLIA HERITAGE SALAD À LA MAUREEN

2 pineapples, sliced lengthwise into 4 halves	1 large apple, cubed
2 cups smoked turkey breast, in chunks	1 cup seedless grapes, halved
1 cup celery, coarsely chopped	1 cup canned pineapple chunks
2 large bananas, thickly sliced	Sauce* Garnish**

Remove pineapple core and discard; remove pineapple meat and set aside for garnish. In large bowl, toss remaining ingredients in sauce, fill pineapple shells, and garnish. Serves 4.
*For sauce: In bowl, combine 1/2 cup mayonnaise, 1/2 cup sour cream, 3/4 cup muscadine preserves, and 2 cups stiffly beaten whipped cream.
**Reserved fresh pineapple, toasted pecans, fresh strawberries, kiwi, and melon in season.

OLD SOUTHERN TEA ROOM

Before the War Between the States, Vicksburg was a thriving shipping center on the Mississippi River. From this point, the state's bountiful cotton was sent north and south, and European goods were shipped up from New Orleans.

During the war, its strategic location high on a bluff gave Vicksburg control over river traffic—any boat passing was subject to fire from Confederate artillery, and the heavily fortified town was secure from attack.

General Grant, with a huge army stranded west of the river, schemed for months to take Vicksburg and separate the Deep South from its western allies. When attempts by land and river were repulsed, Grant sent gunboats down from Memphis by night. Most got through, and transported his army across the river to take Jackson and lay siege to Vicksburg.

For 47 days under Union bombardment, civilians lived in caves, so few lives were lost, but all were nearly starving when

Confederates surrendered on July 4, 1864. The town was under military occupation for thirteen years, and Independence Day was not again celebrated here until 1945.

In Vicksburg's Historic District spectacular antebellum homes are opened for pilgrimages. Volunteer ladies initially prepared food, and Mary McKay opened a tea room in 1941 to carry on the tradition. When its building burned in 1987, The Old Southern Tea Room was re-opened in former dining rooms in The Vicksburg, an apartment conversion of the 1929 Hotel Vicksburg, which was placed on the National Register in 1979.

Here you'll find "plantation" cooking at its finest; many of the original cooks still provide split pea soup, stuffed baked ham, fried chicken, fried Mississippi farm catfish, and lavish Southern vegetables, including turnip greens, corn pudding, sweet potato pone, and blackeyed peas, served with hot biscuits and corn muffins.

Save room for dessert, however. You won't want to miss tipsy pudding, pecan pie, and luscious Down in Dixie Bourbon Pie in a chocolate crust.

Old Southern Tea Room, 801 Clay Street, Vicksburg, is open for lunch 7 days a week, 11:30 a.m. to 2 p.m., and for dinner Monday through Saturday, 5:30 to 9:00 p.m. (601)636-4005. Dress is casual, all legal beverages are served, and reservations are requested for parties of 5 or more. Busiest time is during Pilgrimage (end of March and early April). AE,MC,V. ($)

OLD SOUTHERN TEA ROOM
SWEET POTATO PONE*

6 medium sweet potatoes
2 cups sugar
1/4 cup butter or
  margarine
3 eggs, well beaten
1 teaspoon nutmeg

1 teaspoon allspice
1 teaspoon cinnamon
1 teaspoon ground cloves
12-ounce box white raisins
2 cups milk

Peel and cook potatoes in slightly salted water until tender. Drain thoroughly and beat, then add remaining ingredients. Place in greased casserole; bake 45 minutes at 350 degrees.

*From OLD SOUTHERN TEA ROOM COOK BOOK. Vicksburg, Mississippi. Used by permission.

121

THE MENDENHALL HOTEL
Home of the Original Revolving Tables

T he little farming community of Mendenhall was enlivened by the coming of the railroad, and a 2-story frame hotel built in 1915 accommodated workers on the Illinois Central line from Gulfport to Jackson. Engineers, brakemen, firemen and switchmen who had rooms in the hotel returned for dinner, then played checkers in the lobby.

Annie Belle and Frank Heil, proprietors, in order to feed everyone with a minimum staff, used the lazy susan concept. The difference here is size; enormous round tables seating 18 are almost covered by "revolving tables" laden with traditional Southern fare.

The Heil Hotel was sold to Mrs. Heil's brother, W. H. Goodwin, in 1924. During World War II, the German-sounding name was changed to "The Mendenhall Hotel," but the tradition continued, and after Mr. Goodwin died in 1944, his daughter and son-in-law, Mr. and Mrs. C. Fred Morgan, bought the hotel. They were succeeded in 1979 by their son and his wife; Fred and Nattilie Morgan are the fourth owners, the third generation of the same family, to operate the hotel.

They provide the old-fashioned food and hospitality that

have made the hotel famous all over the world. Platters of steaming hot fried chicken, chicken and dumplings, meat loaf, pork sausage, pork chops, or fried Mississippi catfish alternating with yams, blackeyed peas, greens, okra, butter beans, salads, and homemade biscuits and corn bread—often 25 or 30 dishes on the table at once—are rapidly replenished.

Strangers become fast friends as the food whirls past; regulars teach techniques for reaching what you need without toppling your ice tea, and by the time you enjoy peach, apple, blueberry, huckleberry, or blackberry cobbler, you're ready to stagger to a rocker on the shady porch, just as others have done for generations.

The Mendenhall Hotel is in downtown Mendenhall, just off US 49, 30 miles southeast of Jackson, and is open for dinner 11 a.m. to 2 p.m., Sunday through Saturday, and for supper 6 to 7:30 p.m. Monday through Saturday. From Labor Day to Easter, no meals are served on Monday. (601)847-3113. No alcoholic beverages are served, dress is casual (no tank tops or hats) and reservations are accepted for groups of 15 or more. No charge cards are accepted. ($)

MENDENHALL HOTEL RICE CASSEROLE

1/4 pound margarine or butter
4 green onions, chopped
2 16-ounce OR 3 10-ounce cans cream of mushroom soup

4-ounce can mushrooms, drained, reserving liquid
4 cups cooked white rice
Grated sharp cheese
1 cup toasted chopped almonds (optional)

In saucepan, melt butter and sauté onions until brown. Add soup and mushroom liquid and blend. Place rice in casserole dish; pour soup mixture over, then layer cheese, mushrooms and almonds. Bake at 350 degrees until sizzling hot. Serves 10.

THE POMPOUS PALATE

During the steamboat era, Natchez reached a level of wealth perhaps unequaled in the South, and those who had grown rich were eager to display their success. Outstanding (frequently ostentatious) examples of nearly every early architectural style were built: Spanish Colonial, Créole, Georgian, Raised Cottage, Greek Revival, Gothic Revival, Italianate, Steamboat Gothic, Colonial Revival, and interesting combinations of styles.

The War Between the States halted building—in at least one case, before a house was completed—but Natchez surrendered to the Union early in the war, without the damage caused by bombardment, battle, or long siege. Oddly, the poverty that followed the war and Reconstruction saved old buildings by preventing remodeling that might have altered them beyond reclaim, and Natchez was left a repository of extraordinary antebellum architecture.

Early Pilgrimages in the 1930s created great enthusiasm for preservation, and Natchez today has five historic districts and numerous buildings on the National Register.

In 1904, McDonald and Soulé designed a fine Renaissance

Revival building for the Prentiss Club, an exclusive men's organization. Placed on the National Register in 1979, it was chosen by Loveta Byrne for a restaurant in 1989.

This energetic woman operated another restaurant in a historic building; it was sold when she and her husband acquired The Burn, one of Natchez' famous homes, for a bed and breakfast. With partner Shelley Dearing, who does the desserts, she now serves intelligent, basically Southern food at the Pompous Palate as well.

The menu changes every two weeks, but might offer quail or duck with a praline corn bread dressing, Crawfish Enchiladas with corn relish, or marinated beef tenderloin with herb butter. Side dishes include corn pudding, squash casserole, and stuffed fresh tomatoes.

Shelley's desserts could be Caramel-nut Cheesecake, White Chocolate Mousse pie with fresh berries, or Baked Fudge Pudding with Vanilla Sauce, topped with whipped cream and toasted pecans.

The Pompous Palate, 211 North Pearl Street, Natchez, is at the corner of Jefferson, and is open Wednesday through Saturday, 6 to 10:30 p.m., and on Sunday during Pilgrimage (March and October). (601)445-4946. All legal beverages are served, most men wear coat and tie, and reservations are suggested. Busiest time is during Pilgrimage. AE,MC,V. ($$$)

THE POMPOUS PALATE BAKED CATFISH

6 catfish filets
12-ounce can
  evaporated milk
2/3 cup freshly grated
  Parmesan cheese
1 1/4 cups flour
1/2 Tablespoon salt
1 teaspoon Greek
  Cavender's or
  Italian seasoning

1 Tablespoon paprika
1 teaspoon onion powder
1 teaspoon pepper
1/2 teaspoon
  baking powder
1/2 cup margarine,
  melted with
  1/2 cup butter
Toasted pecans
  or almonds

Marinate catfish overnight in canned milk. Combine next 8 ingredients; dredge fish in mixture and place on greased baking sheet. Drizzle with butter mixture and bake at 400 degrees 20 minutes; do not turn. Top with nuts. Serves 6.

SCROOGE'S RESTAURANT

Long before Europeans came to this country, Natchez was The Grand Village of The Great Sun, ceremonial center for the Natchez Indians. The French, who built Fort Rosalie in 1716, were massacred by the Natchez in 1729, and retaliated by exterminating the tribe. Ceded to Great Britain in 1763, the area was taken by the Spanish in 1779, when the town was laid out much as it exists today.

In 1798, it became capital of the Territory of Mississippi, and was incorporated as an American city in 1803.

The first steamboat arrived in 1811, and thereafter shipment of cotton was more profitable; large landholders made fabulous fortunes as cotton planters, and built opulent mansions in town and on outlying plantations.

By mid-19th century, Natchez had achieved a high standard of wealth and culture, with a stable middle class. About 1864, The York Hotel and Restaurant was built on Main Street. The three-story brick structure was enlarged about 1904 to house the Natchez Printing and Stationery Company on the main floor; a succession of other businesses, among them Earl

Norman's Photographic Studio, occupied the second floor. As part of the Natchez On-Top-of-the-Hill Historic District, it was placed on the National Register in 1980.

When the print shop vacated the building in 1983, it was renovated to become Scrooge's Restaurant, an inviting, informal pub with cozy wooden booths and walls lined with old paneled doors. There is additional seating in the upstairs studio, an appealing open area with fireplaces and white woodwork, and Norman's enlarged photographs of Natchez are used throughout the restaurant.

Scrooge's menu features good cuts of meat, hearty sandwiches, award-winning chili, and lots of salads and appetizers for lighter appetites. The daily special might be grilled pork chops, with blackeyed peas and superb corn bread, or you could choose grilled catfish or Shrimp Ebenezer (broiled, with angel hair pasta).

For dessert, there's candy-like Fudge Brownie Pie, cheesecakes, Mississippi Mud Cake, or creamy rich Butterfinger Pie.

Scrooge's Restaurant, 315 Main Street, Natchez, is open 11 a.m. to 11 p.m., Monday through Saturday. It is also open Sundays during Pilgrimage and at Christmas. (601)446-9922. Dress is casual, all legal beverages are served, and reservations are requested for parties of 8 or more. Busiest times are during Pilgrimage (March and October), and at Christmas. AE,DC,MC,V. ($)

SCROOGE'S BUTTERFINGER PIE

Chocolate crust*   8-ounce carton
1 envelope gelatin   whipping cream
1/2 cup milk   3 Butterfinger candy bars
20 marshmallows   Grated chocolate

Dissolve gelatin in cold milk; heat milk to dissolve completely, add marshmallows and melt. Cool mixture. Whip cream and crush butterfingers. Mix with marshmallow mixture and pour into chocolate crust. Top with grated chocolate, and refrigerate until serving time. Serves 8.

*For chocolate crust: Crush 18 chocolate cookies, blend with 3 tablespoons margarine, and press into 9" pie pan.

MARY MAHONEY'S OLD FRENCH HOUSE RESTAURANT

The Native Americans who called themselves "Biloxis" believed white giants had built mounds along the shore, and would someday return. Spain and France had claimed the area, but it was not until 1699 that a party of Frenchmen settled on the bay of Biloxi at what is now Ocean Springs. They were welcomed by the Indians and lived peacefully among them.

Under subsequent English, Spanish, and American control, the Gulf Coast continued to grow. Unhealthy conditions at "Old Biloxi" prompted establishment of "New Biloxi" in 1820. It soon became a summer resort. When the railroad arrived in 1869, local seafood packed in ice was shipped north, attracting winter tourists.

Biloxi, plagued by hurricanes, has lost most of its antebellum structures; its oldest documented dwelling was built about 1835 for François Gustave Aimé Brunet. The one-and-a-half-story brick Greek Revival cottage with parapet gables originally had four downstairs rooms. On its undercut front gallery is a Greek Revival iron railing identical to that in the Old Capitol in Jackson.

Known for generations as "The Old French House," the little house under the ancient live oak became a restaurant in 1964 and was placed on the National Register in 1984.

The restaurant, originated by the late Mary Mahoney, is now operated by family members, who present the same mixture of Créole and Continental cuisine, emphasizing local seafood. Notable here are a flavorful oyster soup, Lobster Georgo (in cream sauce with brandy, mushrooms, shrimp, and cheese), Broiled Speckled Trout, spicy Baked Stuffed Shrimp, and enormous steaks.

Key Lime Pie, Praline Cheesecake with caramel syrup, and bread pudding with rum sauce are among irresistible desserts.

Mary Mahoney's Old French House Restaurant is at 138 Magnolia Mall, Biloxi, just 3 blocks east of I-10. It is open from 11 a.m. to 10 p.m., Monday through Saturday, plus occasional Sundays. (601)374-0163. All legal beverages are served, dress is casual, and reservations are accepted. AE,DC,MC,V. ($$$)

MARY MAHONEY'S OLD FRENCH HOUSE BREAD PUDDING WITH RUM SAUCE

6 eggs	2 teaspoons vanilla
1/2 teaspoon cinnamon	10 ounces French bread
1 Tablespoon nutmeg	1 1/2 cups seedless raisins
1/4 cup sugar	2 sticks butter, melted
2 cups milk	Rum Sauce*
1/2 cup half and half	

In bowl, mix eggs and spices; add next 4 ingredients and mix well. Break bread in bite-sized pieces into 1 1/2 quart baking dish. Toss with raisins and butter. Pour mixture over and bake 30 minutes, or until golden. Serves 12.

*For Rum Sauce: In saucepan, melt 1 stick butter; blend in 6 Tablespoons flour. Add 2 1/2 cups scalded milk and 3/4 cup sugar. Cook slowly until thick; beat in 4 well-beaten eggs and remove from heat. Add dash each cinnamon and nutmeg, 1 teaspoon vanilla, 1 teaspoon rum flavoring, and 1 ounce rum. Serve over pudding.

NORTH
CAROLINA

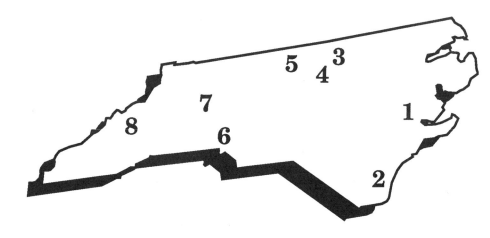

1. NEW BERN
   Henderson House
2. WILMINGTON
   Riverboat Landing Restaurant
3. DURHAM
   Claire's
4. PITTSBORO/CHAPEL HILL
   **The Fearrington House Restaurant
   and Country Inn**
5. WINSTON-SALEM
   Old Salem Tavern
6. CHARLOTTE
   Pewter Rose Bistro
   Alexander Michael's
7. HICKORY
   The Vintage House Restaurant
8. ASHEVILLE
   Gabrielle's at Richmond Hill Inn
   The Grove Park Inn and Country Club

HENDERSON HOUSE

Baron Christophe Von Graffen-
reid, a Swiss, chose land at the confluence of the Trent and
Neuse rivers for a settlement in 1710, and named it for a canton
in Switzerland. Major streets were laid out in a cross, and a town
grew from that point.

Its central location on the coast and accessibility to interior
settlements appealed to Governor William Tryon, who determined to establish a permanent capital at New Bern.

Begun in 1767, the opulent building nicknamed "Tryon's
Palace" was opened in December, 1770. It was residence and
government building of colonial and state governors for a de-
cade; after a period of neglect and disuse, it burned in 1798, and
was reconstructed from original plans in the 1950s.

The Palace and its complex of restored houses encouraged
local preservation efforts, and the original town boundaries now
correspond with the New Bern Historic District, placed on the
National Register in 1973.

One of the most unusual structures in the district, the two-
and-a-half story dwelling occupied by the Henderson House
restaurant was probably built by Durand Hatch about 1818. It

is of brick with a central hall; of New Bern's 50 remaining Federal-style houses, all but two are of frame construction, and most have side halls.

Spare interiors of palest gold show off white Greek Revival moldings, and paintings by Robert Weaver, father of chef/owner Matthew. White napery, pewter tableware and service plates, and dark comb-backed chairs suggest an earlier time, but the cuisine, with a bow to the region, is modern and Continental.

The Carpetbagger, an Australian invention, is a 16-ounce Certified Angus steak stuffed with oysters; veal chops come with a chanterelle (wild mushroom) sauce, and popular Seafood Casserole mingles oysters, shrimp, crabmeat and fish in a wine-butter sauce.

Unusual soups (cold apricot!), special salads at lunch, and desserts such as frozen Coco Moco Pie and delicate White Chocolate Mousse guarantee a satisfying experience.

Henderson House, 216 Pollock Street, New Bern, is open Wednesday through Saturday. Lunch is 11:30 a.m. to 2 p.m.; dinner is 6 to 9 p.m. (919)637-4784. All legal beverages are served, reservations are requested, and reasonably casual dress is accepted, although most men wear coat and tie. AE,MC.V. ($$$)

HENDERSON HOUSE SOUR CREAM MUFFINS

4 ounces unsalted butter
1 1/2 cups sugar
1/2 teaspoon salt
1 1/2 cups sour cream

4 eggs, beaten
Vanilla
2 3/4 cups flour
1 teaspoon baking soda

In mixer bowl, cream first three ingredients thoroughly. By hand, beat in sour cream, then eggs and vanilla. Sift dry ingredients together and fold into mixture. Spoon into paper cups lightly coated with cooking spray. Bake at 475 degrees 15 minutes or until brown. Yields 24.

Chef Matt's tip: add berries in season, chopped apples, or dates; dredge in some of the flour and stir in last.

THE RIVERBOAT LANDING RESTAURANT

Independent Carolinians deposed six governors between 1663 and 1729, when the colony was sold to the English crown. In 1730, Carolina was divided into North and South, and two years later the port town of Wilmington was settled.

In the Spring of 1765, Governor Tryon had hardly taken office when he learned that Parliament had passed the Stamp Act. This unpopular law required colonists to pay a tax on newspapers and all legal papers, including ship clearances, and the Cape Fear economy, linked to shipping, was threatened.

Furious townspeople held a mock funeral for Liberty; Stamp Act advocate Lord Bute was hanged in effigy; and Dr. William Houston, newly appointed stamp collector, was forced to resign. No tax was collected, and the law was repealed in 1766.

Across the street from Houston's humiliation, a succession of commercial buildings were ignited by sparks from steamboats on the Cape Fear River. A portion of the present structure was a wholesale grocer's in 1852; rebuilt in 1879 following a fire, it housed, over time, a boarding house, Penny's Haberdashery, a warehouse, and The Union Restaurant. After damage and vacancy, it was extensively repaired in 1979, and is once again a restaurant.

As part of the 200-block Wilmington Historic District, it was placed on the National Register in 1974.

Downstairs, Riverboat Landing is informal, with large windows and exposed brick; upstairs dining rooms have romantic balconies and spectacular views of the river. Both have the same great food—fresh Tidewater seafood, charbroiled marinated filets, hand-cut veal, and pastas with seafood sauces.

Giant sandwiches and gourmet burgers appear at lunch with daily specials and super salads; desserts anytime are incredible. Chocolate Rum Cake is SOAKED in dark rum, and Mud Pie is chocolate crust filled with chocolate chip ice cream and smothered with fudge sauce.

Riverboat Landing Restaurant, #2 Market Street, Wilmington, is open from 11:30 a.m. until 1 a.m. Monday through Saturday, and from 5 p.m. to 1 a.m. Sunday, with continuous service. (919)763-7227. All legal beverages are served, including Sunday, dress is casual, and reservations are accepted. AE,CB,DC,MC,V. ($$$)

RIVERBOAT LANDING CIOPPINO

3 stalks celery,
   cut thin on the bias
2 carrots, in julienne
1 onion, in 1" pieces
2 cloves garlic, minced
1 Tablespoon hot pepper
   sauce or Tabasco
1 cup white wine

14 1/2-ounce can
   whole tomatoes,
   crushed by hand
8 ounces clam juice
1 teaspoon
   chopped parsley
2 quarts water
Seafood*
Pinch tarragon

In large pot, combine all ingredients except seafood and tarragon. Bring to a boil, then simmer 10 to 15 minutes or until vegetables are softened. Add seafood and simmer until seafood is done—5 to 8 minutes. Do not overcook! Serve in soup bowls and sprinkle with tarragon. Serves 4 to 6.
*crab meat, shrimp, scallops, oysters, cubed fish, whole or chopped clams; any assortment

CLAIRE'S

$\rm T$he country crossroads of Prattville refused right-of-way to the North Carolina Railroad in 1852. Dr. Bartlett Durham offered land a few miles away; a town grew up around the railroad, and town and county were named for him. Incorporated in 1867, Durham grew rapidly, due to the industry of the Duke family, who formed the American Tobacco Company.

Another prominent family, the Mangums, had a farm at what is now Durham's "Five Points" business district. During the 1870s boom, William Mangum turned his farm into a complex that manufactured building materials.

William's son Bartlett grew up in the business, gradually relocating the woodworking plant to eighty acres on the edge of town. By 1913, his operation included a brick factory and a cotton gin.

The two-and-a-half story Neoclassical-style frame house he built near his business in 1905 reflected his wealth and showed the millwork of his lumber yard: elaborate mantels, paneled wainscot, molded baseboards, and fine detail. It was placed on the National Register in 1989.

After Mangum's death in 1927, his land was subdivided, but two daughters lived in the house until 1956. Since then, serving as a dwelling, a church for civil rights activists, and a clothing store, it has been remarkably preserved.

Margaret Pless, a school teacher with a head for business, bought the lovely old house and created a popular restaurant with a leisurely Edwardian pace and food as tasteful as its surroundings.

Grilled quail are brushed with tarragon mustard, lamb steaks are marinated in Red Zinfandel, and butterflied beef tenderloin is stuffed with pâté and spinach. Appetizers, pastas and salads are inventive, and inspired desserts might be cheesecake, homemade pie, fresh fruits in season, sorbet or mousse. And there's "always something chocolate."

Claire's, 2701 Chapel Hill Road, Durham, may most easily be reached off US 15-501 business route. Turn left at exit for NC 751. First right is Pickett Road; after 2 blocks it intersects with Chapel Hill Road in front of Claire's, which is open 7 days a week, 5 to 10 p.m., to 10:30 weekends. (914)493-5721. All legal beverages are served, including Sunday, most men wear coat and tie, and reservations are accepted, requested for groups of 5 or more. AE,MC,V. ($$$)

CLAIRE'S
ROASTED MINT AND GREEN CHILI CHICKEN

1 fresh frying chicken
Salt and pepper
1/2 cup fresh mint
  and rosemary

1 carrot
Green Chili Pesto*

Salt and pepper cavity of chicken; place herbs and carrot inside, and roast 1 1/2 hours at 350 degrees or until juices run clear. Top with Green Chili Pesto and brown under broiler.

*For Green Chili Pesto: In blender or food processor, place 2 cloves garlic, 2 1/2 cups grated Parmesan cheese, 1 cup pine nuts, 8 ounces green chilies, 1/2 cup cilantro leaves, 1/2 cup fresh basil leaves, juice of 1 lemon, and 6 Tablespoons olive oil. Purée until smooth; yields enough for 4 chickens.

FEARRINGTON HOUSE RESTAURANT AND COUNTRY INN

North Carolina's Piedmont has historically been agricultural, with industrial cities, but recent proliferation of academic and research institutions has led to an unprecedented intellectual climate and growth.

Within minutes of Chapel Hill's cultural resources, Fearrington Village is a carefully developed 1200-acre residential park, clustered around shops, an inn, and a farmhouse that has been one of the South's great restaurants since 1980.

The original land grant of 640 acres, taken up in 1786, passed down through Jesse Fearrington's family. The house burned about 1926, and a new house was built. Additions over the years have produced a rambling structure with a dozen or so cozy downstairs rooms.

Fearrington gave up his dairy farm in the mid-1970s, and R. B. and Jenny Fitch bought it. After studying English country villages, R. B. began construction of the first houses, and Jenny decorated, then opened the restaurant.

She did the initial cooking, but a succession of notable chefs has followed, maintaining the restaurant's reputation. "We try to use things around us, and from the region," Jenny said, "using classical methods to prepare them." Menus change daily for the fixed-price, four-course meal, but Southern herbs and ingredients, many from Fearrington's gardens, are incorporated.

Think about Chilled Tomato Dill Soup swirled with cream, Braised Veal topped with Lemon Oregano Gravy, and Grits Timbale, rich with sharp cheddar.

The house Chocolate Soufflé, moist and pudding-y with thick chocolate sauce, is the only dessert ALWAYS offered, but whatever you choose, you can't go wrong.

Fearrington Village is 8 miles south of Chapel Hill on US 15-501. The restaurant is open Tuesday through Saturday, 6 to 9 p.m., 5:30 to 7:30 p.m. on Sunday. (919)542-2121. Beer and wine are available, including Sunday after 12:00 noon; jackets are required for men, and reservations are strongly suggested, especially in mid-May and during football season. There are 14 overnight rooms. MC,V. ($$$)

FEARRINGTON HOUSE FRESH FRUIT WITH GRAND MARNIER SAUCE**

1/2 cup sugar	4 ounces green or
1 1/2 cups water	black grapes
1 Tablespoon lemon juice	1 cantaloupe
2 Tablespoons	1/2 honeydew melon
Grand Marnier	1 pineapple
2 or 3 oranges	1 starfruit (optional)
3 or 4 kiwi	Grand Marnier Sauce*

Dissolve sugar in simmering water and cool. Add lemon juice and liqueur. Peel and slice oranges and kiwi; halve grapes and chunk remaining fruit. Add to syrup and chill; serve with Grand Marnier Sauce*. Serves 6 or 8.
*For Grand Marnier Sauce: In double boiler over VERY low heat, cook and stir 4 or 5 egg yolks and 1/3 cup sugar about 10 minutes, until thick. Cool. Whip 8 ounces heavy cream until soft peaks form; combine with yolks and liqueur.

Chef's Note: Substitute fruits according to season. Those that discolor (peaches, apples, bananas) must be added at the last minute.

**From THE FEARRINGTON HOUSE COOKBOOK. Copyright 1987 Jenny Fitch, Chapel Hill, North Carolina. Used by permission.

OLD SALEM TAVERN

Gerrman-speaking Moravians, Protestants seeking religious freedom, bought 100,000 acres in Carolina in 1753, and named it "Wachau" (later "Wachovia"), for a place in Austria.

Their first two settlements were farming communities, but Salem, established in 1766, was a trade and craft center. Each shop, privately owned, was under church control, and no poor-quality items were allowed.

The ordered, productive life of the Moravians attracted many friends (Governor Tryon was one), and in 1772 they constructed a tavern (George Washington slept there) to house them. After a fire, it was rebuilt in 1784, and its success required an annex in 1816.

In 1849, Moravians sold land north of Salem for a county seat; named for a hero of King's Mountain, Winston's growth from tobacco and textiles overtook Salem, and the two were consolidated in 1913.

Well-preserved by the Moravians, and restored by a community program begun in 1950, much of Old Salem is open to the public. The village was placed on the National Register in 1966.

In the yellow and green tavern annex, restored in 1969, waitresses in Moravian dress bring hot pumpkin muffins and rolls while guests study the menu. A few Moravian dishes appear—wedges of flaky pastry overstuffed with savory chicken, spicy gingerbread with lemon curd ice cream—with rack of lamb in rosemary crumbs, duck topped with mustard basil butter, Cajun steak and shrimp, and Chocolate Amaretto Pie.

Everything, including bratwurst, breads, and ice creams, is made on the premises, fresh every day, by a staff as quality conscious as the Moravians.

Old Salem Tavern, 736 South Main Street, Old Salem, Winston-Salem, is open 7 days a week. Lunch, Sunday through Friday, is 11:30 a.m. to 2 p.m., Saturday until 2:30; dinner, Monday through Thursday, is 5 to 9 p.m., Friday and Saturday until 9:30. (919)748-8585. All legal beverages are served, including Sunday after 1 p.m., coat and tie are not required, and reservations are recommended for dinner, and for 6 or more at lunch. AE,MC,V. ($$)

OLD SALEM MORAVIAN GINGERBREAD

2 1/4 sticks softened
  unsalted butter
2 cups sugar
3 eggs
1 cup molasses
1/3 cup finely chopped,
  peeled fresh ginger
Rind of 2 oranges, grated

1 teaspoon cinnamon
1/8 teaspoon ground cloves
1 teaspoon baking soda
1 Tablespoon
  cider vinegar
3 1/2 cups sifted flour
1 cup milk

In large bowl, beat butter and sugar until fluffy, adding eggs one at a time. Mix in next 5 ingredients in order; in small dish, stir together soda and vinegar, then add to mixture. Add flour and milk alternately, stirring just enough to blend. Spread batter in greased and floured 9" x 13" x 2" pan, and bake at 375 degrees 55 to 60 minutes or until it pulls away from side of pan. Cool in pan on wire rack. Cut into 16 squares, serve with homemade lemon ice cream.

PEWTER ROSE BISTRO

Settlers of the area that would become Charlotte came up from Charleston, down from Pennsylvania, and west from Virginia, converging in 1748. Primarily Scotch-Irish, German, and English in origin, they declared their allegiance to England by naming county and city for George III's wife, Charlotte of Mecklenburg.

By 1775, however, the independent spirit that would characterize the state had asserted itself.

The Mecklenburg County Convention was in session in Charlotte when news came of the battles of Lexington and Concord; already distressed about taxes and British interference in local government, irate members demanded independence, and issued the Mecklenburg Declaration of Independence the following day.

Many believe this to be the first such declaration of freedom; the date, May 20, 1775, appears on the North Carolina flag and State Seal.

Charlotte experienced amazing growth as a textile, financial, and distribution center. When new residential areas were needed, Edward Dilworth Latta, streetcar entrepreneur, developed "streetcar suburbs" southeast of uptown Charlotte.

In Dilworth, laid out in 1891, a two-story free-standing warehouse, once part of the Nebel Hosiery Mill, is now office and retail space, and upstairs, the Pewter Rose Bistro.

Its open, airy area, gentled by hangings and art, is ideal for serious food in a casual, comfortable setting. California ideas and French techniques combine in an exciting fashion: grilled grouper is marinated in soy, ginger, and sweet vermouth; smoked chicken breast and andouille sausage are sautéed in gorgonzola cream; and Big Easy Sauté tops tomato fettuccine with Créole seafoods and tasso (Cajun ham).

There are daily cheesecakes (chocolate chip peanut butter topped with ganache), "everyday" chocolate rum cake, and Mocha Brûlée, silky, creamy, possibly the best chocolate mousse you'll ever taste.

Pewter Rose Bistro, 1820 South Boulevard, Charlotte, is open for lunch Monday through Friday, 11:30 a.m. to 2 p.m., for dinner 5:30 to 10 p.m. Thursday, 5:30 to 10:30 p.m. Friday and Saturday. (704)332-8149. All legal beverages are served, dress is casual, and reservations are accepted only for parties of 6 or more. AE,MC,V. ($$)

PEWTER ROSE DEVONSHIRE CREAM
WITH CRIMSON SAUCE

1 teaspoon plain gelatin	1 1/2 teaspoons vanilla
3/4 cup cold water	8-ounce carton sour cream
1 cup whipping cream	Crimson Sauce*
1/2 cup sugar	

Soften gelatin in water, heat until dissolved, cool. In large bowl, beat cream with sugar and vanilla until soft peaks appear; don't over beat. Combine with gelatin and sour cream and pour into serving dishes. Spoon Crimson Sauce over to serve. Serves 6 to 8.

*For Crimson Sauce: In saucepan, combine 4 teaspoons shredded orange peel, 1/4 cup orange juice, 1 1/2 cups whole fresh cranberries, and 1 1/3 cups water. Bring to a boil; simmer 15 minutes. Add 1/2 cup sugar and 1/2 cup cranberries, cook 5 minutes more or until cranberries pop. Cool; cover and chill. Yields 1 cup.

ALEXANDER MICHAEL'S

In the American Revolution, the battle of Camden, South Carolina, was a rout. Overconfident Major General Horatio Gates pitted exhausted patriots against British veterans under Cornwallis. Although outnumbered, the British over-ran Gates' men, who sped into the darkness, outstripped by their commander.

Fleeing toward Charlotte, Gates encountered Major William Davie, of Waxhaw, bringing as reinforcements a battalion of cavalry he had equipped with his own money. Gates, pursued by Cornwallis, continued his flight, but Davie harried Cornwallis' troops, then defended Charlotte's Courthouse against great odds before retreating in good order to Salisbury.

Gates was removed from command; Davie was promoted to Colonel, and later served in Congress, was Governor of North Carolina, and Ambassador to France.

Not far from the courthouse site Davie defended so bravely, Charlotte's 19th Century textile prosperity is reflected in the Fourth Ward, a residential area of varied Victorian styles. In this park-like setting, residents have restored many handsome homes—and one neighborhood grocery.

The E. W. Berryhill grocery and general store served its community for 70 years. Later use as paint store, thrift shop, and delicatessen did not harm the fabric of the structure; lovingly adapted in 1983, it retains its original appearance and friendliness as a neighborhood tavern.

And the food is good. Spicy Herb Potato Soup topped with cheddar has a hint of dill; hearty burgers and sandwiches are made of honest ingredients, individually prepared; and after five p.m., entrées include fresh seafoods, pastas, and HOT blackened chicken over red beans and rice.

Alexander Michael's, 401 West 9th Street, Charlotte, is on the corner of Pine, and is open Monday through Saturday from 11:30 a.m. with continuous service. Dinner is 5 to 11 p.m. (704)332-6789. All legal beverages are served including a wide variety of domestic and imported beers, dress is comfortable—ties are discouraged—and reservations are not accepted. AE,MC,V. ($$)

ALEXANDER MICHAEL'S
ROASTED RED PEPPER SOUP

4 Tablespoons butter
1 large onion, chopped
2 cloves garlic, chopped
4 shallots, chopped
2 Tablespoons flour
46-ounce can tomato juice
2 cups chicken stock
 or canned chicken broth
1/2 teaspoon cayenne
 pepper (or to taste)

1/4 teaspoon white pepper
28-ounce can tomatoes,
 with juice
2 cups heavy cream or
 half and half cream
5 large red peppers,
 roasted and peeled
1 cup Cabernet Sauvignon
 (or to taste)

In large pan, sauté onion, garlic, and shallots in butter until soft; stir in flour and cook over low heat 2 or 3 minutes. Add tomato juice, stock, and seasonings. Simmer 5 minutes and remove from heat. In food processor, purée tomatoes, alternating with cream, red peppers, and soup mixture. (May require several batches.) Return puréed soup to pot, correct seasonings, and add wine. If soup is too thick, thin with any of the above liquids. Serves about 15.

VINTAGE HOUSE RESTAURANT

Stagecoaches, crossing the Piedmont from the mountains, stopped as early as 1784 at Hickory Tavern; the town of Hickory Station grew up around the tavern. Its first industry, based on the rich timber of the area, was Piedmont Wagon Company.

Other early industries, made possible by the railroad, were mining and manufacturing of iron products, cotton and cord mills, and production of such lumber-based products as shingles, window sashes and blinds, and furniture.

By 1910, downtown Hickory could boast electric lights, its own bank, and a full city block of commercial buildings.

Albert Abernethy, a hardware merchant, built a two-story, Shingle-style home in his parents' pasture in 1913. The style, new to the South although popular in New England, was characterized by diamond-pane leaded-glass windows and fine interior millwork.

In 1947, a Mr. Bothwell bought the house, adding an open veranda and stone steps to a sunken garden. It remained in his family until 1981, when Glenda Schenk opened the Vintage House. She enclosed the porch and veranda, carefully matching

146

construction and moving leaded windows from upstairs to unify the façade.

The house's gracious interior is an appropriate setting for the innovative, yet classic food. Grouper is wrapped in lacy potatoes, as is sautéed lamb; prawns, sea scallops and shrimp wontons are steamed in soy-ginger butter; and filet steaks rolled in black and rose pepper are flamed in brandy.

Among popular desserts are baked rice pudding, crème caramel, cheesecakes, and fresh fruit with Crème Anglais, but some regular visitors won't leave without the moist, delicious fudge pie.

The Vintage House, 271 Third Avenue, Northwest, Hickory, is on the corner of Third Street, and may most easily be reached from NC 127 North. Turn on Third Avenue; restaurant is 3 blocks, on the right. Lunch, Monday through Friday, is 11:30 a.m. to 2 p.m.; dinner, Monday through Saturday, is 6 to 10 p.m. (704)324-1210. All legal beverages are served, dress is "dressy casual," and reservations are preferred. AE,MC,V. ($$$)

VINTAGE HOUSE TURKEY PICCATA

4 cutlets (8 ounces) sliced raw boneless breast of turkey	CLARIFIED butter OR oil for sautéing
1/2 cup flour	Salt and white pepper
1 egg, beaten with 1 Tablespoon water	Wine butter sauce*
	Cooked pasta

Pound cutlets lightly, dust in flour, dip in egg wash, and sauté in skillet, adding salt and pepper. Cook about 2 minutes on each side, until light brown. Blot with paper towels and place on warmed plate. Top with wine butter sauce and serve with pasta. Serves 2.

*For Wine Butter Sauce: Place 2 ounces white wine and 1 ounce lemon juice in skillet with 1 shallot, minced. Reduce over medium heat until almost dry; add 4 ounces cream and reduce until slightly thickened. Remove from heat, whisk in 1/2 pound softened unsalted butter and salt and pepper to taste. Any extra sauce may be used over vegetables.

GABRIELLE'S AT RICHMOND HILL INN

Cherokee hunting grounds on the plateau that is now Asheville were protected by the British; no settlements were allowed in the mountains until 1776.

A town laid out in 1794, eventually named for Governor Samuel Ashe, became a regional trading center. After the railroad arrived in 1880, industrial development increased, and Asheville's future as a summer resort was assured.

In 1889, Richmond Pearson built a spectacular Queen Anne-style house on a hill above the French Broad River. A two-and-a-half story frame structure with a hip roof, lower cross gables, and a wrap-around porch, it expressed the Victorian ideal at its finest. Richmond Hill was placed on the National Register in 1984.

Pearson had a distinguished diplomatic career, then retired to practice law in Asheville. The house remained in his family until 1974, when it was sold to North Carolina Baptist Homes for a retirement home.

Preservationists encouraged the group to use the house, and even purchased adjacent land and offered it in exchange, but the church group went ahead with plans for demolition.

Finally, they agreed to sell the house—if it was moved. It required $100 thousand and a week's strenuous work to move the house 600 feet; it weighed 1.5 million pounds.

Purchased by The Education Center, of Greensboro, who also bought an adjoining 40 acres, the house was meticulously restored to become an inn and conference center in 1989.

Gabrielle's, named for Pearson's beautiful wife, occupies the dining room and glass-enclosed porch. In this nostalgic framework, exquisite American and Nouvelle cuisine are served with Southern warmth and charm.

Your dinner might be Duck Consommé with Wild Mushrooms; Grilled Marinated Shrimp on angel hair pasta with pesto; Chicken Breast Roulade, filled with spinach and pine nuts; and, for dessert, mountainous Chocolate Volcano.

Gabrielle's at Richmond Hill Inn, 87 Richmond Hill Drive, Asheville, is most easily reached off I-240. Exit 19/23, then exit 251. Turn left off ramp; at first stoplight, left on Riverside Drive, then right on Pearson Bridge Road. Cross bridge, turn right on Richmond Hill Drive to top of hill. Lunch, Monday through Friday, and Sunday brunch are 11 a.m. to 2 p.m.; dinner is 6 to 10 p.m. every evening. (704)252-7313. There are 12 overnight rooms at Richmond Hill Inn. AE,MC,V. ($$$)

GABRIELLE'S GRILLED NORWEGIAN SALMON WITH DILLED BERRY RELISH

2 kiwi, diced
4 large strawberries, diced
1/3 cup fresh blueberries
1/4 cup fresh raspberries
2 Tablespoons
  chopped fresh dill weed
1 Tablespoon sugar
1 Tablespoon lemon juice
4 6-ounce filets
  Norwegian salmon
Lemon twists and
  sprigs of dill for garnish

Combine first 7 ingredients in a bowl and toss delicately; chill 2 hours. Grill salmon over open flame or on gas grill until cooked but still moist. Arrange on 4 plates, top with relish, and garnish with lemon twist and dill. Serves 4.

GROVE PARK INN AND COUNTRY CLUB

Patent medicine king E. W. Grove found Asheville's mountain climate so healthful that he bought land on Sunset Mountain and built a resort. Asheville had been known throughout the South as a place to escape summer heat, but Grove's vision was larger: he wanted an extraordinary hotel that would attract wealthy and influential people from all over the world.

Patterned after the inn in Yellowstone Park, and designed by Grove's partner and son-in-law, Fred Seely, the massive structure was built of huge boulders from nearby mountains, all carefully placed to show their weatherbeaten side.

Enormous fireplaces, focal points of the Great Hall, burned 12-foot logs, requiring andirons weighing 500 pounds each, and the rest of the hotel was built on the same immense scale. Each room had a view of the mountains, solid oak Craftsman-style furniture, and Irish linen curtains and spreads. Environment and food were wholesome and conducive to rest, and when William Jennings Bryan delivered the opening address in 1913, he became the first of thousands of illustrious visitors. Grove Park Inn was placed on the National Register in 1973.

Purchased in 1955 by Charles Sammons, the hotel embarked on a restoration/renovation plan which still continues. The adjoining country club and golf course were added in 1976, and wings were added in 1984 and 1988 for additional overnight rooms.

Now a world-class, year-round resort with every amenity, the Grove Park Inn maintains the same high standards of comfort and service Mr. Grove decreed.

And, weather permitting, you can still dine on the open-air Sunset Terrace, enjoying a delectable four-course meal, served to music, as you watch the sun sink into the misty mountains.

The Grove Park Inn, 290 Macon Avenue, Asheville, may be reached by the Charlotte Street exit (5-B) off I-240. Drive north half a mile, turn right on Macon to top of hill. There are several restaurants at the inn; Sunset Terrace is the only one entirely in the original structure. It is open seasonally, serving lunch through October, 4-course fixed-price dinner through September. (704)252-2711, (800)438-5800. All legal beverages are served, including Sunday, jackets are required, and reservations are strongly recommended. There are 510 overnight rooms. AE,DC,MC,V. ($$$)

GROVE PARK INN
BISQUE OF CLAM AND CHICKEN

2 ounces butter
1/4 cup flour
2 cups clam juice
1 cup chicken stock
1 cup light cream
1 cup heavy cream

1/4 cup finely
  chopped onion
1/4 cup diced celery
1/2 cup diced chicken
1/2 cup diced clams
Salt and pepper

In large saucepan, melt butter and stir in flour. Add clam juice and stock and stir until boiling. Add remaining ingredients and simmer 20 to 30 minutes. Serves 8.

SOUTH
CAROLINA

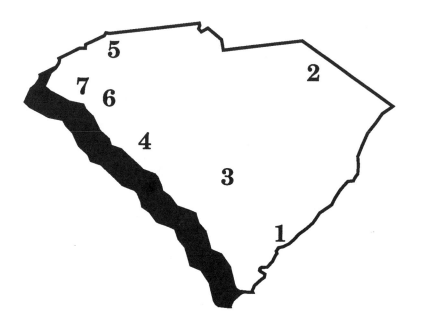

1. CHARLESTON
   The Primerose House
   82 Queen
2. FLORENCE
   Bonneau's
3. COLUMBIA
   California Dreaming
4. ABBEVILLE
   The Belmont Inn
5. GREENVILLE
   Seven Oaks Restaurant
6. ANDERSON
   Morris Street Tea Room
7. PENDLETON
   Liberty Hall Inn

THE PRIMEROSE HOUSE

Founded in 1670, Charles Town was laid out in a grid fronting on the Cooper River, with fortifications on three sides. Above the settlement, land grants became suburbs as growth required.

A portion of Isaac Mazyk's 1720 land grant was purchased in 1758 by Christopher Gadsden, merchant, planter, and revolutionary radical. A delegate to the Stamp Act Congress and both Continental Congresses, he commanded South Carolina's Revolutionary forces, and served 30 years in the General Assembly.

Recovering land his father had lost at cards, Gadsden reclaimed marshes by digging a canal; in 1767 he built what was for many years the largest wharf in America.

Across the street from Gadsden's home, a 2-story brick and stucco house was built in 1817 by Robert Primerose, a vendue master or auctioneer. A Charleston "single house," its gable toward the street, one room wide and two rooms deep, with piazzas on the south side, it is unusual in having an elaborate semi-circular portico in its gable end. As part of the Charleston Historic District, a National Historic Landmark, it was placed on the National Register in 1978.

In its English basement, a distinguished restaurant enjoys simple surroundings. Chef/owners Joanne Yaeger and Mickey Glennon prepare "everything from the ground up," using their imaginations and childhood recollections for unusual, savory combinations. British and Hungarian flavors recur, but theirs is primarily very special Southern food.

Chilled white peach/passion fruit soup has a hint of fennel; fried grits are sauced with mushroom ragoût, brunch omelets are filled with jambalaya and okra; and free-range veal is sautéed with white grapes and vermouth.

The Primerose House, 332 East Bay Street, Charleston, is open 7 days a week. Breakfast, Tuesday through Friday, is 8 to 11 a.m.; lunch, Tuesday through Friday, and Sunday brunch are 11:30 a.m. to 2 p.m., and dinner, Tuesday through Thursday and Sunday, is 6 to 10:30 p.m., to 11:30 p.m. Friday and Saturday. (803)723-2954. All legal beverages are served, including Sunday after 1 p.m., dress is casual to formal (less dressy outside) and reservations are preferred for dinner, not accepted other times. No parties over 8 seated. AE,MC,V. ($$$)

PRIMEROSE HOUSE SAVORY CHEESECAKE PACKED IN PEPPERCORNS

1 1/2 pounds cream cheese	1/4 teaspoon salt
6 ounces chevre cheese	1/4 cup
5 medium eggs	chopped fresh herbs
1 1/4 cups sour cream	(chervil, chives, basil)
2 Tablespoons	Bread crumbs
cider vinegar	1/4 cup cracked OR coarse-
1 teaspoon lemon juice	ground black pepper

In large mixer bowl, beat cheeses until smooth. Add eggs one at a time, scraping bowl after each. Do not over beat; leave mixture thick. Fold in sour cream, then next 4 ingredients. Oil a 10" springform pan; dust liberally with crumbs and pepper. Pour batter into pan; sprinkle with mixture and bake at 350 degrees 50 minutes. Cool; run knife around rim; remove. Serve with crackers, garlic toasts, or fruit.

82 QUEEN

I n her three hundred years, Charleston has survived earthquakes, hurricanes, fires, poverty and war. Irregular patterns of destruction and rebuilding account for different architectural styles, but after each calamity, the city's indomitable spirit has recreated one of the loveliest cities in the world.

Since the beginning, storms, fires, earthquakes and hurricanes have struck Charleston at least every 20 years. Some were truly devestating, but Charlestonians can take anything in stride.

Descriptions seem remarkably dispassionate, except for accounts of the "great fire of 1861," that swept across the peninsula, covering 540 acres, and the earthquake of 1886 that damaged 90 per cent of Charleston's buildings. Hurricane Hugo, of recent memory, seems tame in comparison.

Queen Street was burned out in 1861. A 3-story brick single house built at #82 in 1869 was reduced to 2 stories by the earthquake. It was repaired in 1888 to match #84, but extensive remodeling in 1974 obscured façades of both.

The restaurant established in 1982 includes #82, #84, and

a carriage house, surrounding a lush courtyard where meals are served, weather permitting. And such meals! Geared around local seafood and updated regional "Low Country" foods, 82 Queen's cuisine is inimitable.

Barbecued shrimp are basted in Southern Comfort, quail are sauced with peanuts, and fried okra has Japanese-style breading. Here you'll find home-sun-dried tomatoes; imported pineapples; and pond-raised shrimp, catfish, and striped bass. Desserts are great; the key lime pie is PERFECT.

82 Queen, 82 Queen Street, Charleston, is open 7 days a week. Lunch is 11:30 a.m. to 2 p.m.; dinner is 6 to 10 p.m., to 10:30 p.m. Friday and Saturday. (803)723-7591. All legal beverages are served, dress is "nice casual," and reservations are suggested. AE,MC,V. ($$)

82 QUEEN LOW COUNTRY SHRIMP OVER HOPPIN' JOHN RICE

3 cups water
1 1/2 cups chicken stock
2 cups Uncle Ben's rice
2 Tablespoons butter
1 teaspoon salt
1 cup dried field peas
6 cups water
1 piece smoked pork
1 teaspoon chopped garlic
Salt and pepper

1/2 cup chopped kale
1 small yellow onion, chopped
3 Tablespoons butter
4 pounds fresh shrimp
1 medium red onion
2 red peppers
1 bunch chives, chopped
3 teaspoons butter

In large pot, bring water and stock to a boil. Add rice, butter, and salt; simmer 20 minutes or until water is absorbed. Spread on cookie sheet and refrigerate. In large pot, combine peas, water, pork and garlic. Season with salt and peper. Cook 2 hours or until beans are just tender. Strain beans and refrigerate. Sauté kale and onion in butter until onions are transparent; add peas and rice and sauté until very hot. Peel and devein shrimp. Julienne onion and peppers. Sauté in butter until shrimp are done. Spoon over rice on a large platter. Serves 8.

BONNEAU'S

The Wilmington and Manchester Railroad constructed a station in a stand of pines in northeastern South Carolina; joined by the Northeastern Railroad in 1853, and the Cheraw and Darlington in 1859, the junction became a town named for the baby daughter of General William Wallace Harlee, head of the Wilmington and Manchester.

During the War Between the States, Florence's railroads made it a shipping center for goods and troops, later a hospital town and site of a prison for captured Federals.

Shops built in 1868 by the Northeastern Railroad added to the town's growth, and when the Atlantic Coast Line also established shops and began taking over other lines, Florence became a distribution center for the region.

Among the town's prosperous families was the Irby Family, known for dry goods. Their fine house, a two-story red brick vernacular Prairie-style structure, was built about 1900 on the tree-shaded street named for them. Purchased in 1923 by the Early family, it became a tourist home called "The Lantana Inn." It was again a residence before being converted to a restaurant in 1975 by Bonneau Lesesne, who owned the Greenbrier restaurant next door.

When a bank bought and demolished the Greenbrier in 1983, Bonneau's remained the only house on what had been a handsome residential street. Its steak house menu and the Greenbrier's were combined to become an upscale restaurant where individually prepared fresh foods are served in comfortable wood-paneled rooms.

Popular here are scampi, slow-cooked roast prime rib, and petit frogs legs; shrimp are offered in five different preparations, and the day's catch may be prepared to order blackened, poached, or broiled. Quail, veal, steaks, and, frequently, rack of lamb, are always well received, and desserts often include Chocolate Meringue Pie, Chocolate Torte, and White Chocolate and Rocky Road Cheesecakes.

Bonneau's, 231 South Irby Street, Florence, is open for dinner Monday through Saturday, 6 to 11 p.m. The lounge, with a bistro menu, is open from 4 p.m. to 12:00 midnight. (803)665-2409. All legal beverages are served, dress is "dressy casual," and reservations are preferred. Busiest time is during races at nearby Darlington Race Track, Thursday through Saturday on Memorial Day and Labor Day weekends. AE,DC,MC.V. ($$)

BONNEAU'S BROCCOLI BONNEAU

10-ounce package
  frozen chopped broccoli
Salt and pepper
8 ounces sour cream
Juice of 1 lemon

1/4 teaspoon
  crushed oregano leaves
1/4 cup melted butter
1/4 teaspoon salt
4 fresh medium tomatoes

Cook broccoli according to package directions; season with salt and pepper, and drain. Add remaining ingredients, and mix thoroughly. Scoop out insides of tomatoes and heat shells in oven; fill with broccoli mixture. Serves 4.

CALIFORNIA DREAMING

After the Revolution, South Carolina needed a centrally located capital city. The site chosen was "Taylor's Hill" above the Congaree River. Columbia was laid out with wide streets to prevent epidemics, and the first session of the Legislature met in 1790.

The town grew rapidly. South Carolina College opened in 1805, canals, roads, and railroads improved communication, and by 1860, Columbia was a polished little city of 8,000 people.

In December of that year, a convention met in Columbia to draw up the Articles of Secession; by April, war was inevitable. A munitions plant, a Confederate mint, hospitals, and other war-related activities swelled Columbia's population, as did evacuees from coastal areas.

General W.T. Sherman, after his destructive march from Atlanta to Savannah, continued to Columbia. By accident or intent, the city was burned to the ground, leaving 20,000 homeless.

So Columbia is a "new" town. Reconstruction was difficult, but by the turn of the century, the textile industry had helped to restore the town's economy.

The Union Station, a project of the Southern Railway and the Atlantic Coast Line Railroad, was built in 1902. A distinguished yellow brick building with elements of several styles, it was placed on the National Register in 1973, and was restored in 1983 to become a restaurant famous for good food at a reasonable price.

Spacious and light, California Dreaming is a "fun" place for people of all ages. Open kitchens send out aged beef steaks and half-pound burgers; barbecued baby back ribs; fresh fish and chicken breasts; and Mexican and Italian items. Salads are in frozen bowls, milkshakes have real ice cream, and Apple Walnut Cinnamon Pie is aptly described as "out of control."

California Dreaming, 401 South Main Street, Columbia, is open from 11 a.m., 7 days a week; Monday through Thursday, it is closed 3 to 5 p.m.; Friday, closed 3 to 4:45 p.m. Saturday service is continuous, to 11 p.m., and Sunday to 10 p.m. (803)254-6767. All legal beverages are served, dress is "appropriate," and reservations are not accepted. Busiest times are football weekends and graduation at the University of South Carolina. AE,MC,V. ($$)

CALIFORNIA DREAMING'S PROCEDURE FOR ROASTING PRIME RIB

David Howard, Director of Food and Beverage for MSJ Corp., makes these suggestions to approximate California Dreaming's tender, juicy prime rib: Go to a specialty meat market or butcher, if possible, and request aged (C.D. beef is 21 days, minimum) beef with more marbling than usual.

Trim excess fat and net or tie at 1" intervals, or ask butcher to do this—keeping meat in its shape promotes even cooking. Season and place in preheated 250 degree oven; after 60 minutes, reduce heat to 140 degrees for a MINIMUM of 4 hours for an 8 to 11 pound prime rib. Low temperature tenderizes meat and keeps flavor. Meat thermometer in center of meat should register 140 degrees for medium rare. Yields 15 to 20 servings.

BELMONT INN

Andrew Pickens, an early set-
tler and Indian fighter, later a Revolutionary War hero, built a
fort that was the beginning of Abbeville; he made his spring
available for public use as the neighborhood developed. By
1795, the town had a post office and served as county seat.

With the arrival of the Greenville and Columbia Railroad in
1853, many fine houses were constructed, and business was
conducted around a square. Far-seeing farmers formed an
agricultural society in 1859, proposing a diversified crop system; this preserved the soil and was not so dependent on slave
labor as cotton farming.

Between 1872 and 1895, several severe fires destroyed
many of the buildings on the square; rebuilding, with early 20th
century additions, resulted in tree-shaded Court Square Plaza,
surrounded by the Courthouse, the Opera House, many commercial structures, and the Eureka Hotel.

The two-story brick hotel, incorporating a number of styles,
with a full basement and 40 rooms, cost $30 thousand, and
opened in 1903. In 1938, it was renamed "The Belmont Hotel,"
and continued to provide rooms for travelers and performers at

the Opera House until it closed in 1972. As part of the Abbeville Historic District, it was placed on the National Register in 1972.

The hotel was purchased in 1983, and renovated to become the Belmont Inn, with 24 rooms decorated in antiques and reproductions, and good food in the Heritage Dining Room.

Chef Bruce Robinson has been with the Inn since its opening, offering Southern-flavored French food. Popular Pecan Chicken is baked with a Dijon sauce; homemade soups include Carolina She-Crab (he-crabs don't have roe) and Italian chicken; and tennis-ball sized rolls are cloud-like.

A favorite dessert is Zuccotto, a trifle-like creation of pound cake, whipped cream, chunks of chocolate and bourbon.

Belmont Inn, 106 East Pickens Street, Abbeville, is on Court Square, and is open 7 days a week. Breakfast is 7 to 9 a.m., 8 to 10 weekends; lunch is 11:30 a.m. to 2 p.m.; and dinner is 6 to 9 p.m., to 10 p.m. weekends; no dinner is served on Sundays. (803)459-9625. All alcoholic beverages are served, except Sunday, dress is casual, but coat and tie are usual, and reservations are encouraged. There are 24 overnight rooms. AE,DS,MC,V. ($$$)

BELMONT INN BLACKEYED PEA SOUP WITH COLLARD GREENS

2 1/2 cups blackeyed peas
3/4 cup salt pork, diced
3/4 cup onion, diced
1 clove garlic, minced
2 teaspoons flour
3/4 cup potatoes,
  peeled and diced

8 cups water
1/8 teaspoon
Worcestershire sauce
1 bunch collard greens,
  washed and chopped
1 bay leaf, crumbled
Salt and pepper

Pick over peas, wash, and soak 4 hours or overnight; drain. In large pot, try out pork; sauté onions and garlic in rendered fat. Stir in flour and cook five minutes. Add remaining ingredients, bring to a boil, and simmer 1 hour or until peas are tender. Adjust seasonings. Yields 3 quarts.

SEVEN OAKS

E ven before the Revolution, when lands along the Reedy River were Cherokee territory, Richard Pearis (or Paris) came from Virginia to trade with Indians and build a mill, the first of many industries in the area.

A Loyalist, his lands (estimated at 10 or 12 square miles) were confiscated. In 1788, 400 acres were purchased by Lemuel J. Alston, brother of Governor Joseph Alston.

Alston built a home on Prospect Hill, established a town called "Pleasantburg," then sold his holdings in 1816 to Vardry McBee, who built one of the earliest cotton mills. By 1831, renamed "Greenville," the town had several industries powered by the river; with McBee's encouragement, Furman University relocated in Greenville in 1851, and the town was reached by rail in 1853.

Furman's theological department became the Southern Baptist Theological Seminary and moved to Louisville, Kentucky, in 1859, but among memories left behind are streets in Boyce Lawn Subdivision named for its faculty members.

Developed in 1889 on the grounds of James Boyce's home, this area of handsome houses was eagerly sought by leaders in the textile industry. The Pettigru Street Historic District was placed on the National Register in 1982.

Built by the Grahame Family, the Neoclassical-style house now occupied by Seven Oaks restaurant changed hands frequently, and stood empty until a 1981 restoration. Wraparound porches, 14-foot cove ceilings, parquet floors, and intricate millwork create an intimate, romantic setting for food described by Chef Robert Hackl as "American Freestyle."

Lighter, healthier entrées are prepared using every technique—broiled, poached, grilled, etc.—and feature the highest quality ingredients. Local seafoods, homemade breads, and shiitake mushrooms grown by the restaurant appear on a menu that changes seasonally.

Striking presentation enhances broiled amberjack with a beurre blanc sauce, garnished with caviar; pork tenderloin is served in pesto with blackeyed peas and sun-dried tomatoes; and Chicken Seven Oaks is sauced with artichoke and lobster béchamel.

Recurring desserts are creamy flans; "light" cheesecakes; Chocolate/Pineapple Napoleon, and Deep Dish Toll House Cookie, served warm with ice cream, fudge sauce, and whipped cream.

Seven Oaks, 104 Broadus Avenue, Greenville, is open for lunch 11:30 a.m. to 2 p.m., Monday through Friday, and for dinner 6 to 10:30 p.m., Monday through Saturday. (803)232-1895. All legal beverages are served, most men wear coat and tie, and reservations are suggested. AE,MC,V. ($$$)

SEVEN OAKS
CREAM OF SHIITAKE MUSHROOM SOUP

1 onion, diced
1 leek, diced
Butter for sautéing
3 pounds
  shiitake mushrooms
4 shallots, diced

1 clove garlic, minced
2 ounces marsala wine
1 quart chicken stock
1 cup heavy cream
Chopped parsley
  for garnish

Sweat onion and leek in butter; add next 3 ingredients and cook until soft. Deglaze pan with marsala; reduce to half and add stock. Cook 30 minutes; purée, add cream and strain.

MORRIS STREET TEA ROOM

General Andrew Pickens frequently rode from Abbeville to his home, "Tamassee," in Oconee County. When Anderson County was created in 1826, the courthouse was located along the "General's Road."

As the county seat, Anderson grew rapidly, reaching a population of 500 by mid-century. Nancy Caldwell, a widow, bought four acres in 1851, and built a raised cottage, typical of coastal houses, for her home. The main floor is 12 feet over a full basement, believed to afford protection from mosquitoes.

Mrs. Caldwell died in 1853, and her estate sold the house to Dr. William Bullein Johnson, chancellor of Johnson Female Seminary (later University) and first president of the Southern Baptist Convention. When ill health forced him to return to Greenville, Dr. Johnson's home was sold to Margaret Morris, another widow, whose four daughters had attended the Seminary.

Mrs. Morris died in 1883, and two of her daughters lived in the house until their deaths. When the last one died in 1928, the house was divided into two apartments. Rescued by preservationists in 1971, it was restored and furnished, and for several years was open to the public as a museum house. The Caldwell-Johnson-Morris Cottage was placed on the National Register in 1971.

In 1980, caterer Angie Finazzo opened the Morris Street Tea Room in the house. Chicken Crêpes and individual quiches are popular at lunch; men like the Union Jack sandwich (shaved ham and smoked turkey on open French roll topped with Mornay Sauce and smoked bacon strips).

Dinner choices include Veal Continental, with pea pods and shrimp; marinated broiled lamb chops; grouper sauced with crab meat, and medallions of tenderloin sautéed with artichoke hearts and topped with Béarnaise.

Many choose Shu Shu à la Créme for dessert: French pastry filled with creamy lemon mousse.

Morris Street Tea Room, 220 East Morris Street, Anderson, is open for lunch Tuesday through Friday, 11 a.m. to 2 p.m., and for dinner Friday and Saturday, 6 to 10 p.m. (803)226-7307. All legal beverages are served, dress is "dressy casual" and reservations are requested for dinner. AE,DC,MC,V. ($$)

MORRIS STREET TEA ROOM
CANADIAN CHEDDAR CHEESE SOUP

12 ounces grated cheddar cheese
1 1/2 Tablespoons cornstarch
10 ounces water
3/4 teaspoon salt
1/4 teaspoon white pepper
3/4 teaspoon Worcestershire sauce
Pinch garlic powder
1/2 cup diced cauliflower
8 ounces mushrooms, sliced
1/3 cup diced carrots
8 ounces onion, diced
1/2 cup diced smoked ham
1 ounce butter
2 cups half and half cream

Mix cheese and cornstarch; heat water to boiling. Add cheese to water a little at a time, stirring constantly; cook until melted and smooth. Add next 4 ingredients. Sauté next 4 ingredients in butter until tender; add to soup, and while heating, stir in half and half. Serves 6.

LIBERTY HALL INN

The first town to be settled above Camden, Pendleton, laid out in 1790, was the seat of the Pendleton District, later divided into Anderson, Pickens, and Oconee counties. It was named for Judge Henry Pendleton of Culpeper, Virginia, who organized one of the South's first Revolutionary companies.

Placed at the intersection of two Indian paths, Pendleton was settled by families from Pennsylvania, Maryland, Virginia, and North Carolina. It was for many years the government and business center of the "Up Country," later attracting coastal planters who built lavish summer homes.

In 1815, the Pendleton Farmers Society, an early agricultural reform group, was formed. Their meeting hall and other early 19th-century structures cluster around Pendleton's village green, forming the heart of the Pendleton Historic District, which includes more than 6,000 acres and 50 buildings, and was placed on the National Register in 1970.

A Piedmont plantation-style house was built in the 1840s just outside Pendleton by Thomas and Nancy Sloan. Called "Homeplace," it was a two-story structure of five rooms, with high ceilings and wraparound piazzas on both floors, but was more than doubled in size under a turn-of-the-century owner who operated a boarding house. It was restored to become an inn and restaurant in 1985.

Innkeepers Susan and Tom Jonas present four-course dinners, price determined by entrée, of "inspired country dining." Menus change daily, depending upon availability of fresh ingredients, but beef, seafood, veal, chicken, and trout are prepared and sauced with imagination.

Choices of several hot or chilled soups; fruit or vegetable salads; and desserts such as Bread Pudding with Custard Sauce, fresh fruit shortcakes, Apple Crisp, frozen Chocolate Mocha Squares, and Chocolate Sin make dining at Liberty Hall Inn a sure thing.

Liberty Hall Inn, 621 South Mechanic, Pendleton, may most easily be reached from exit 19-B off I-85. Take SC business route 28, inn is 7 miles, on right. It is open for dinner Monday through Saturday, 6 to 9 p.m. (803)646-7500. All legal beverages are served, most men wear coat and tie, and reservations are appreciated. There are 10 overnight rooms. AE,CB,DC,DS,MC,V. ($$)

LIBERTY HALL INN
MARINATED BEEF TENDERLOIN

1/2 cup ruby port wine	1 bay leaf
1/4 cup olive oil	2 pounds boneless
1/4 cup soy sauce	beef tenderloin steaks,
1/2 teaspoon pepper	cut 1 1/2" thick
1/2 teaspoon dried thyme	
1/4 teaspoon hot	
pepper sauce	

In large nonreactive container combine all ingredients except beef; stir well. Add steaks, cover and refrigerate 3 to 6 hours, turning occasionally. (Longer marinating may alter texture of meat.)

In preheated 450 degree oven, heat wire rack in foil-lined baking pan 5 to 10 minutes. Place steaks on rack, bake 7 minutes, turn and bake 7 minutes more. Liberty Hall cooks steaks to 130 degrees, medium rare. Serves 4.

TENNESSEE

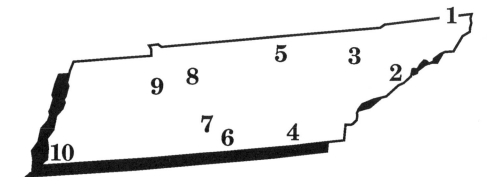

1. BRISTOL
   The Troutdale Dining Room
2. SEVIERVILLE
   Applewood Farmhouse Restaurant
3. KNOXVILLE
   The Soup Kitchen
4. CHATTANOOGA
   Churchill's
5. COOKEVILLE
   Diana's
6. COWAN
   The Corner House
7. LYNCHBURG
   Miss Mary Bobo's Boarding House
8. NASHVILLE
   Mère Bulles
9. DICKSON
   Turn of the Century
10. MEMPHIS
    Café Society

THE TROUTDALE DINING ROOM

In the early 1770s, influenced by hunters' tales of rich lands, pioneers settled north and west of the Holston River. Threatened with Indian attack, the settlers met with three similar groups in 1772 to form the Watauga Association, probably the first attempt at self-government in America. This organization, providing mutual protection from Indians, was the beginning of the state of Tennessee.

Captain Evan Shelby's fort at Sapling Grove, later "King's Meadows," was renamed "Bristol" when a town was laid out in 1852.

Charles Robertson Vance, a Bristol lawyer, requisitioned guns for the Confederate Army during the War Between the States. After the war, he took his family to safety, returning to his home in Bristol when pardoned by President Andrew Johnson.

In the 1890s, Bristol boomed, and the Vance home was remodeled into a Queen Anne frame house with a spreading porch. The original structure was more than doubled by an addition on the right side; the roof was raised and crested with ornamental iron.

The house remained in the family until 1987 when Barry and Carol Serber, looking for a better location for their successful Troutdale Dining Room, bought it and reopened there in June, 1988. Original oak woodwork has been skillfully restored; a corner bay window and four tile fireplaces, fitted with gas logs, evoke the Victorian era.

The Serbers' exposure to diverse ethnic cuisines has resulted in a menu of classic dishes from all over the world, interpreted in Carol's style, and individually prepared. Only the highest quality ingredients are used; some are shipped from New York, fresh herbs are locally grown, and trout are swimming in the former creamery behind the house minutes before they are prepared.

The Troutdale Dining Room, 412 6th Street, Bristol, is open for lunch Monday through Friday, 11:30 a.m. to 2 p.m.; for dinner Monday through Saturday, from 5 p.m. Café provides lunch 11:30 a.m. to 2 p.m.; appetizers, desserts, and coffees 3:30 to 11 p.m. (615)968-9099. Dress is casual, all beverages are served, and reservations are preferred. MC,V. ($$$)

TROUTDALE DINING ROOM CEVICHE

1 pound firm-fleshed
 white fish (halibut,
 orange roughy, etc.)
Juice of about
 8 fresh limes
4 tomatoes, skinned,
 in 1/2" dice
1 large onion,
 very finely diced
1/4 cup fresh minced
 coriander, or to taste
Salt and pepper

1 Tablespoon
 fresh oregano leaves,
 chopped, OR
1 1/2 teaspoons
 dried oregano
2 to 3 cloves garlic,
 minced
1/2 cup thinly sliced
 Spanish olives (optional)
1/2 jalapeño or
 serrano pepper,
 very finely minced
3 avocados, halved

Cut fish into 3/4" cubes; place in nonreactive container and marinate in lime juice to cover. Refrigerate 6 hours to overnight; fish will be opaque when done. Drain lime juice, and add next 9 ingredients, mixing carefully. Refrigerate until ready to serve. Serve in avocado halves. Serves 6.

173

APPLEWOOD FARMHOUSE RESTAURANT

One of the most colorful, romantic characters in Tennessee history, tall, handsome John Sevier (pronounced SeVERE), an early settler, took part in nearly every activity that shaped the territory and the state.

A Virginian of French Huguenot descent, Sevier was brave, friendly, a natural leader. He was an Indian-fighter, hero of the Battle of King's Mountain, Governor of the State of Franklin, General of Militia of The Southwest Territory, four-term Representative to the U. S. Congress, first Governor of Tennessee, and served five additional terms as Governor.

Sevier County and its seat, Sevierville, are named for this dashing patriot. Here, some of the loveliest country in the state is changing from farms to tourism; in keeping with this trend, a restaurant has been developed on a farm overlooking the Little Pigeon River.

Cattle and tobacco were raised here, but an apple orchard proved better use of the land. In 1980, the barn became The Apple Barn and Cider Mill, a retail outlet for apples, country foods and crafts.

In 1986, the 1921 farmhouse was expanded to six dining

rooms, each with its own personality. The original living and dining rooms contain a beautifully crafted mantel, room divider, and cupboards made by Louis Buckner, a black artisan born in slavery. By 1880, he was listed as a cabinetmaker; he also built fine houses in Sevierville, including two on the National Register.

The Applewood Farmhouse Restaurant features, of course, apples—apple juice, tiny hot applesauce muffins, apple fritters, and apple butter—but there's plenty of variety, and everything is down-home good. Meats are smoked on site, and all baked goods are homemade.

Hearty breakfasts provide everything from country ham to buttermilk pancakes; lunch can be fried chicken, fruit salads, or "Farmburgers"; and dinner adds entrées of chicken-fried steak, barbecued spareribs, and rainbow trout. At all meals, be sure to save room for dessert: apple cake, apple roll, and Applewood Pie-Cake, topped with whipped cream and rum sauce.

Applewood Farmhouse Restaurant is on Lonesome Valley Road, Sevierville, and is open 8 a.m. to 9 p.m. Sunday through Thursday, to 10 p.m. Friday and Saturday, with continuous service. (615)428-1222. Dress is casual, and reservations are accepted only for groups of 15 or more. Busiest time is September (Apple Festival) and October. AE,MC,V. ($$)

APPLEWOOD FARMHOUSE APPLE FRITTERS

1 cup milk	1 teaspoon vanilla
1 egg, beaten	1/2 cup sugar
4 Tablespoons margarine, melted	1/2 teaspoon salt
	3 cups cake flour
Juice and rind of 1 orange	2 teaspoons
1 cup coarsely chopped apple	baking powder
	Oil for deep frying

In mixing bowl, combine first 3 ingredients. Add fruit and vanilla. Sift dry ingredients and stir into mixture only until blended. DO NOT OVER MIX. Preheat oil to 350 degrees. Drop fritters off end of tablespoon into hot oil and fry, turning to brown evenly. Drain and cool.

175

THE SOUP KITCHEN

In 1786, Captain James White built a log cabin on the west side of First Creek; it became a provisioning place for Revolutionary War veterans who came to take up their land grants.

William Blount, Territorial Governor, arrived in 1790 and named the new town for Secretary of War Knox, hoping for help against Indian attack. As Knoxville grew, retail stores were established, and in 1853, land was given for a public market. In 1897, a large brick building was erected on the site, replacing earlier wooden structures.

Peter Kern, a German immigrant, settled in Knoxville and established a bakery on Main Street about 1872, and an ice house in 1878. By 1890, he was mayor of Knoxville, and had built a three-story bakery adjacent to the Market House. Mr. Kern died in 1907, and after the business was sold in 1925, it was relocated. Several businesses were housed in the Kern Building, which was placed on the National Register in 1982.

After widespread concern for sanitation and a serious fire in 1959, the Market House was demolished. Today, Market Square is again an open air market, with fountains and shrubbery that make it a favorite noontime gathering spot.

In the Kern Building, a restaurant called "The Soup Kitchen" serves lunch to hundreds by utilizing a unique format: only soups, salads, and breads are sold, in a fast-moving cafeteria-style line. Even those with a half-hour lunch break can be assured of wholesome, delicious food—fast.

What makes it special is three-fold: the first-class quality of the food, the homespun comfort of the restaurant, and the friendliness and enthusiasm of the staff.

Chili is always one of the seven or eight daily soups; four specialty salads are offered daily, and four or five breads, one of which is a sweet bread. Desserts are equally special, and the only problem here is choosing.

The Soup Kitchen, #1 Market Square Mall, Knoxville, is open 11 a.m. to 2 p.m., Monday through Friday. Carry out and delivery are available in downtown Knoxville. (615)546-4212. Dress is casual, bottled beer is served, and no credit cards are accepted, although personal checks are. Busiest time is Dogwood Arts Festival, three weeks in April. ($)

THE SOUP KITCHEN GRATIN SAVOYARD

6 Tablespoons butter	4 cups water
1 bunch leeks, coarsely cut	1 pound cream cheese
1/2 teaspoon white pepper	1 pound vanilla yogurt
4 cups chicken stock	1 pound frozen
1/2 cup flour	chopped spinach

In large pan, melt butter and sauté leeks with pepper. Add chicken stock. Whisk flour into water and strain into stock. Add cream cheese and yogurt, and beat until smooth with wire whisk. Add spinach. Serves 8 to 10.

177

CHURCHILL'S

The War Between the States left Chattanooga in poor condition; earthworks and forts remained from the hostilities, streets were almost impassible in wet weather, and camp followers lingered, ignored by corrupt politicians.

By 1870, the city government was in control, undesirables had left town, and business was on the increase, encouraged by good transportation and cheap labor. Chattanooga became a thriving manufacturing center, and during the boom of 1888, four businessmen joined to build four connected commercial buildings, sharing a common rock-faced façade, at the corner of Broad Street and Seventh Avenue. Two of them occupied the building: James Trigg's wholesale grocery, and James Smartt's wholesale boot and shoe business.

The building, a furniture store for 67 years, acquired a pink granite façade and a modern interior in 1939. The store was closed in 1985; as the Trigg-Smartt Building, it was placed on the National Register in 1986.

Remodeled for multiple use, the building now houses

Churchill's restaurant, opened in 1987, which achieves the cozy elegance of an English club in a light-filled interior.

Here you'll find food with an English flavor and an attention to detail seldom found. Lunch is from a menu upstairs, but those in a hurry appreciate buffet lunch in the Pub, in what is believed to be the original street level of the building. Churchill's extensive wine collection is housed on the former sidewalk, visible through stone arches.

Dinner offers unusual appetizers, special soups and salads, and entrées that range from Shrimp & Lobster to Rack of Lamb and Medallions of Beef and Veal. An almost overwhelming selection of homemade desserts is presented on a cart, as are cordials, liqueurs, and rare whiskies.

You don't have to be an English clubman to appreciate this kind of food and service!

Churchill's, 701 Broad Street, Chattanooga, is open for lunch Monday through Friday, 11:30 a.m. to 2:30 p.m.; for dinner 6 to 9:30 p.m., Monday through Thursday, to 10 p.m. Friday and Saturday; and for Sunday brunch buffet 11:30 a.m. to 2 p.m. (615)266-4455. All legal beverages are served; dress is casual in the pub, but most men wear coat and tie upstairs. Reservations are encouraged, almost a necessity on Saturday or performance nights. AE,MC,V. ($$$)

CHURCHILL'S RED SNAPPER
WITH GINGER BUTTER

One 7-ounce snapper filet   **1 ounce watercress**
Seasoned flour   **Ginger Butter***
  for dredging
CLARIFIED
  butter for sautéing

Dredge snapper in flour and sauté in CLARIFIED butter. Braise watercress and place on plate, lay snapper on top, and top with 1 ounce Ginger Butter. Serves 1.

*For Ginger Butter: In saucepan, mix 3/4 teaspoon powdered ginger, 2 1/4 teaspoons chopped shallots, 1 1/4 teaspoons lemon juice, and 2 Tablespoons white wine. Boil until reduced by half. Add 1/2 pound butter and stir until melted; remove from heat and beat 1 minute. Yields enough for 6 filets.

DIANA'S
Home of the Sweetest Buns in Town

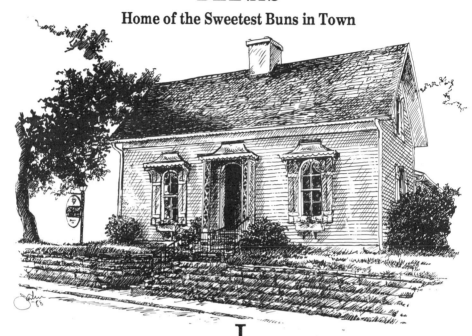

In 18th-century towns, baking was done in bake shops, where housewives took their own loaves to be baked in large ovens. Isolated farms, with hundreds of workers, had bake-houses and full-time bakers.

On the frontier, neither ovens nor flour was available; cooking utensils were few and crude and cornbread was a staple. Removed from the cob, kernels of dried corn were placed in a mortar and pounded with a pestle until fine. Mixed with water, the meal became johnnycake, ash cake, corn pone, or mush, depending upon preparation.

Corn breads were the cheapest and most filling bread, but biscuits, rolls, loaf bread, and sweet breads were soon added. Baking was a necessary, respected skill, and a woman who could bake good bread was a popular hostess.

Diana Lynch opened a restaurant and bakery in a quaint Gothic-revival cottage in 1987. The house was built by Hickman Quarles, a descendent of Major William P. Quarles, whose 1805 settlement at White Plains was the beginning of Cookeville.

Diana's opens early with continental breakfast—freshly baked cinnamon or pecan rolls, a slice of warm coffee cake—but specializes in lunch. The decor is country Victorian, the fragrance of fresh bread is intoxicating, and the food, homemade daily from fresh ingredients, is just fine.

Diana's, 104 East Spring Street, Cookeville, is at the corner of Fleming Street. Take exit 287 off I-40; at the square, turn left on Spring and drive west one block. Bakery opens at 7 a.m.; 8 a.m. on Saturday for full breakfast. Lunch is 11 a.m. to 2:30 p.m., Monday through Saturday. (615)526-6967. Dress is casual, and reservations are accepted for parties of 5 or more. MC,V. ($)

DIANA'S PERFECT WHITE BREAD

2 1/2 cups flour
1 package dry yeast
2 1/4 cups milk
2 Tablespoons sugar

1 Tablespoon shortening
2 teaspoons salt
3 1/4 to 3 3/4 cups flour

In large mixer bowl, combine 2 1/2 cups flour with yeast. In saucepan, heat next 4 ingredients until warm, stirring constantly. Add to dry mixture and beat at low speed for 1/2 minute, scraping sides. Beat 3 minutes at high speed. By hand, stir in enough flour to make a moderately stiff dough. Turn out onto floured surface, and knead 8 to 10 minutes, or until smooth and elastic. Shape into ball and place in greased bowl, turning once to grease top. Cover; let rise in warm place until doubled, about 1 1/4 hours. Punch down; turn out on floured surface; divide in half. Cover and let rest 10 minutes. Shape into two loaves; place in 8 1/2" x 4 1/2" x 2 1/2" loaf pans. Cover and let rise until doubled, 45 to 60 minutes. Bake at 375 degrees about 45 minutes. If tops brown too fast, cover with foil last 15 minutes. Remove from pans and cool on racks.

THE CORNER HOUSE

Although six railroad charters were granted by the Tennessee Legislature in 1831, it was not until 1842 that the first train actually ran; it made a few trips, then was taken over for debt.

In other states, railroads were succeeding; a line was built from Charleston, South Carolina, to the Savannah River, and as it approached Chattanooga via Atlanta, railroad fever rose. Work began on the Nashville and Chattanooga Railroad in 1848, and a tunnel through Sewanee Mountain, believed impossible, was completed February 21, 1851.

This engineering feat required two years of drilling, with only hand drills and black powder to cut through solid rock. When the two ends met, there was great rejoicing, and hundreds marched through the tunnel with lighted candles. The tunnel was 2,228 feet long, and the track leading to it, the steepest grade railroad in the world.

Among the earliest settlers of the Elk River Valley after the War of 1812, the Miller family were farmers and merchants. A depot at the base of the mountain began the town of Cowan in 1852, and one of the Millers built a simple Queen Anne-style cottage in Cowan around the turn of the century.

With its low porch and cutaway bay window, the house appealed to sisters Bobbye Cox and Freida Money, who bought it, decorated it and in 1984 opened "The Corner House."

Here they serve the kind of home cooking most people wish they had at home. Chicken Salad and Chicken Divan are always on the menu, but seasonal changes may result in a creamy cheese soup with bits of pimiento and ham, or orange spice muffins with raisins and orange peel, or perhaps a rum cake dripping with brown sugar, nuts, and cherry glaze. Whatever is available, it'll be freshly made of the freshest ingredients, and it won't be quite like anything you've tasted before. This creative approach to home cooking is worth a trip across the mountain any time!

The Corner House, U.S. 64/41A, Cowan, is 90 miles south of Nashville, about 12 miles off I-24, and is open for lunch 11 a.m. to 2 p.m., Monday through Saturday. (615)967-3910. Dress is casual, although most men wear jackets, and reservations are accepted. It is closed between Christmas and New Year's Day. Busiest time is parents' weekend at The University of the South (Sewanee), 3rd weekend in October. No credit cards accepted, personal checks accepted. ($$)

CORNER HOUSE WHITE GAZPACHO

3 medium cucumbers,   3 Tablespoons vinegar
  peeled and chunked   2 teaspoons garlic salt
3 cups chicken broth   Toppings*
3 cups sour cream

Whirl cucumber chunks in blender with a little broth; combine with other ingredients just enough to mix. Chill. To serve, spoon into dishes and sprinkle with toppings.

*Toppings: 2 tomatoes, peeled and chopped; 3/4 cup toasted almonds; 1/2 cup sliced green onions; or 1/2 cup chopped parsley.

MISS MARY BOBO'S BOARDING HOUSE

Landholder Thomas Rountree laid out Lynchburg about 1818. His cabin, on a choice lot with two springs, was later enlarged; in 1867, owner Dr. E. Y. Salmon built a Greek Revival frame house adjoining the older structure.

Called "The Grand Central Hotel," it housed teachers, single men, and Revenue Agents inspecting Jack Daniel's new distillery, and Mrs. Salmon's hospitality kept her table filled.

When the Salmons retired in 1908, Mary and Jack Bobo took over the business. The Bobo Hotel, as the food's reputation grew, became "Miss Mary Bobo's Boarding House."

Miss Mary operated the boarding house until her death in 1983, at the age of 101. She had stopped renting rooms, serving only the midday meal; when the Jack Daniel Distillery reopened the house after her death, the policy was continued.

Today, Proprietress Lynne Tolley, Jack Daniel's great-great niece, serves Miss Mary's old-fashioned Southern food family style, and presides over one of the five big tables.

Over dinner of fried chicken and another meat, perhaps pot roast or meat loaf, accompanied by six Southern vegetables, often grown in the garden behind the house, plus corn bread, biscuits, or hot rolls, the stiffest stranger unbends.

Hostesses tell stories about Lynchburg's past, explain unfamiliar foods to those from distant parts, and draw amusing anecdotes from guests.

By dessert—possibly fruit cobbler, strawberry shortcake, or burnt-sugar cake with caramel icing—guests have become friends, and plan to return as soon as possible.

You will, too.

Miss Mary Bobo's Boarding House is just off the Lynchburg Town Square, 70 miles south of Nashville and 90 miles west of Chattanooga. It is about 45 minutes from I-24. "Dinner" is served PROMPTLY at 1 p.m., by reservation only. On Saturdays and occasionally during the week, seatings are 11 a.m. and 1 p.m. (615)759-7394. Dress is casual. MC,V, personal checks. ($$)

MISS MARY BOBO'S
LADIES OF LYNCHBURG TEA LOAF*

3 cups flour	1 1/2 cups chopped pecans
1 cup sugar	1 egg
4 teaspoons	1 cup milk
baking powder	1/2 cup
1 1/2 teaspoons salt	Jack Daniel's whiskey
1/4 cup butter	1/4 cup chopped pecans
2 teaspoons	
grated orange rind	

In bowl (or food processor), combine first 4 ingredients, and cut in butter until coarse crumbs. Stir in orange rind and pecans. In small bowl, mix liquid ingredients, and stir into flour mixture just until blended. Turn into greased and floured 9" x 5" x 3" loaf pan and sprinkle pecans over top. Bake about an hour, until toothpick comes out clean. Cool in pan 10 minutes, turn onto rack to cool completely.

*From Jack Daniel's THE SPIRIT OF TENNESSEE, Copyright 1988 Lynne Tolley, Nashville, Tennessee. Used by permission.

MÈRE BULLES

The settlement of Nashborough, on a bluff overlooking the Cumberland River, was the center of seven forts under the Cumberland Compact. Later, the name "Nashville" included all seven sites, and the city was chartered in 1806.

Market Street, a block from the fort, was the focus of business activity, especially after steamboat traffic began. In the 1870s and -80s, large commercial structures were built on the east side of Market Street, with access to river wharves on the other side.

Many of these buildings have striking Italianate cornices and window designs; as a group, they constitute one of the best-preserved examples of Victorian commercial architecture in the country. Market Street became Second Avenue in 1904; the Second Avenue Commercial District was placed on the National Register in 1972.

The largest, most elaborate of these structures was built about 1872, occupied by a carriage maker and a liquor distributor. As a wholesale grocery, it housed Joel Owsley Cheek, developer of the first commercially blended coffee.

Prior to his blend, coffee beans were roasted and ground at home. Combining several types of beans, roasting and grinding them in bulk, Cheek produced a superior, consistent flavor. About 1892, he convinced the Maxwell House Hotel to serve his coffee; President Theodore Roosevelt's praise resulted in the "Good to the last drop" slogan.

Part of the building is again used for foods, beverages, and spirits; in 1987 Mère Bulles (pronounced mare-bulls), a restaurant/wine bar, opened. Its name, French for "Mother Bubbles," quotes the owner's young grandson, who associated his grandmother with champagne.

There is certainly champagne at Mère Bulles, and a Cruvinet system provides 56 fine wines by the glass. Equally challenging is "California-type food with a Continental flair," frequently prepared in or sauced with wine, that fits the romantic mood of the high-ceilinged brick dining rooms, where tall arched windows overlook the Cumberland, and open fires warm a winter night.

Mère Bulles, 152 Second Avenue North, Nashville, is open 7 days a week. Lunch, Monday through Saturday, is 11 a.m. to 2 p.m.; Sunday brunch 11:30-3 p.m. Summer dinner hours are 6 to 11 p.m., Monday through Thursday, to 12:00 midnight, Friday and Saturday, to 10 p.m. Sunday. Winter dinner hours are 5:30 to 10 p.m. Light foods are available between meals. (615)256-1946. All legal beverages are served, dress is "tastefully casual," and reservations are highly recommended, especially on weekends. AE,DC,DS,MC,V. ($$)

MÈRE BULLES BASIL CHICKEN ROTINI

1/2 pound rotini noodles, cooked al denté
Butter for sautéing
1 whole chicken breast, in julienne
1 plum tomato, diced
1 ounce dry white wine
Basil, salt, and pepper
1/3 cup grated Parmesan cheese
1/3 cup heavy cream

In heavy skillet, melt butter and sauté chicken until almost done. Add tomato, wine and seasonings, and reduce by one half. Add cheese and cream, and cook until chicken is tender. Serve over noodles. Serves 3 or 4.

TURN OF THE CENTURY

J ames Robertson, "The Father of Middle Tennessee," was born in Virginia in 1742, and moved to North Carolina at an early age. One of the North Carolina "Regulators," he was a leader of the Wataugans by the time he was thirty. In 1779, he led the overland party to found Nashville.

Head of the court and colonel of the militia under The Cumberland Compact of 1780, Robertson was named Brigadier General for Middle Tennessee by George Washington in 1790, and was a delegate to Tennessee's constitutional convention in 1796.

Between his duties, Robertson found time to establish the Cumberland Iron Furnace in present-day Dickson County about 1793. The furnace produced cannonballs used during the Battle of New Orleans in 1814.

During the War Between the States, Union troops built the Nashville and Northwestern railroad to the Tennessee River. Fourteen miles below Cumberland Furnace, a station was built on the line in 1865; the town that grew up around it was named Dickson.

About 1890, a Queen Anne-style two-story frame house was

built on South Main Street. It was later altered by the addition of a two-story porch and some interior woodwork, but remains a gracious example of its period.

In March, 1983, JoAnn and Harold Sutton opened the Turn of the Century Tea Room on the first floor, then added on the "Garden Room." This open, airy area with an outdoor feeling is now the main dining room; three Victorian rooms are used for overflow and private parties.

Menus reflect the season, and generous portions are the rule. Entrées are prepared to order, with fragrant muffins and homemade light bread, and desserts range from Miss Anna's yellow loaf cake with burnt-sugar frosting to Hot Fudge Pudding Cake oozing its own sauce and topped with ice cream.

Turn of the Century Tea Room, 303 South Main Street, Dickson, opens for luncheon groups by appointment; dinner, Friday and Saturday, is 5 to 9 p.m.; and Sunday lunch buffet is 11 a.m. to 2 p.m. Hours may expand—call for information. (615)446-7300. Dress is casual, reservations are preferred for dinner, and busiest time is "Christmas in the Country" arts and crafts festival the first weekend in November. AE,DS,MC,V, Personal Checks. ($$$)

TURN OF THE CENTURY
MULBERRY GARDEN CASSEROLE

One 6-ounce box
Uncle Ben's Long Grain
and Wild Rice
One 2-ounce jar pimiento,
drained
One 15-ounce can
French-style green
beans, drained
One 5-ounce can sliced
water chestnuts, drained

2 teaspoons
finely chopped onion
One 10 3/4-ounce can
Campbell's Cream
of Celery soup
(no substitute)
1 cup Miracle Whip
salad dressing
2 cups cooked,
diced chicken

Mix all ingredients well, but gently, so as not to break up the beans. Bake 30 minutes at 375 degrees.

CAFÉ SOCIETY

I̶n 1900, Memphis established a "City Beautiful" program, laying out 335 acre Overton Park, and creating a scenic parkway to encircle the city. With trolleys into the suburbs and automobile traffic, planned residential neighborhoods boomed between 1900 and the mid-1920s.

In the Evergreen Historic District, placed on the National Register in 1985, well-maintained houses exemplify architectural styles popular during the period. One of the few commercial structures in the district is a one-story brick veneer business row with a flat roof, built near Poplar Avenue about 1920. It was used for offices and shops, but by the late 1970s had deteriorated into used appliance stores. Michel Leny (pronounced Lenny), son of a Belgian chef, came to Memphis in 1966. Encouraged to become a hairdresser, he operated his own salon, but yearned for a restaurant.

In 1987, he rescued two end shops in the Evergreen row to become "Café Society." Bright and airy at lunchtime, it is romantic in the evenings, with candles and flowers on pink tablecloths. The casual, pleasant feeling is fostered by the staff, many of whom were present on opening day.

Food here is International, emphasizing Belgian home cooking, French favorites, and inventions of Michel and his father. Wonderful soups are served in hard rolls, and at lunch, eight entrée items (fish, meat, pasta, etc.) are prepared a different way every week.

Popular desserts include frosty ice cream Brandy Alexanders, and a fat cream puff filled with French vanilla ice cream, dripping with Belgian chocolate.

Café Society, 212 North Evergreen, Memphis, is open for lunch 11:30 a.m. to 2 p.m. Tuesday through Friday, for dinner 5 to 10 p.m. Tuesday through Thursday, to 11 p.m. Friday and Saturday. Sunday brunch is 11:30 a.m. to 2 p.m. (901)722-2177. All beverages are served, dress is casual, and reservations are accepted. AE,MC,V. ($$)

CAFÉ SOCIETY OYSTERS MAURICE

1/2 pound chopped raw shrimp	3 Tablespoons flour
6 Tablespoons butter, divided	1 egg yolk, beaten
	1/4 teaspoon white pepper
2 dozen oysters	1 teaspoon salt
1/2 to 1 cup milk	1/4 cup bread crumbs
2 Tablespoons white wine	1/4 cup grated Gruyère cheese

In skillet, melt 2 Tablespoons butter, add shrimp, and cook 2 to 3 minutes. Set aside. Pour oyster liquor in measuring cup and add milk to make 1 3/4 cups. Stir in wine. In heavy skillet, melt remaining butter, stir in flour, and whisk. Cook over high heat until boiling and slightly thickened. Reduce heat and simmer 3 minutes. Blend 1/4 cup sauce with beaten egg yolk, then add mixture to skillet. Add seasoning, remove from heat, and stir in shrimp.

Fill baking dish with rock salt and place oyster shells on it. In each shell, spoon one Tablespoon of shrimp sauce, top with oyster and additional spoon of sauce. Sprinkle with bread crumbs and cheese. Broil, 3 inches from flame, 1 or 2 minutes, or until brown. Serves 4.

VIRGINIA

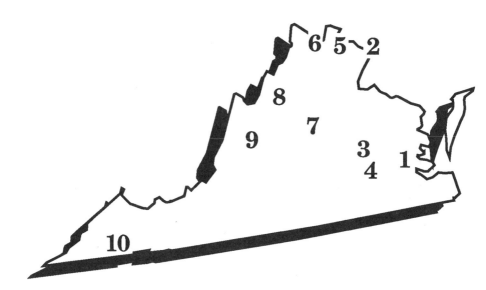

1. WILLIAMSBURG
   Shields Tavern
2. ALEXANDRIA
   Gadsby's Tavern
3. RICHMOND
   Mr. Patrick Henry's Inn
4. PETERSBURG
   The French Betsy
5. MIDDLEBURG
   The Red Fox Inn
6. BERRYVILLE
   Battletown Inn
7. CHARLOTTESVILLE
   The Old Hardware Store Restaurant
8. HARRISONBURG
   **The Joshua Wilton House Inn
   and Restaurant**
9. LEXINGTON
   The Willson-Walker House Restaurant
10. ABINGDON
    Martha Washington Inn's First Lady's Table

SHIELDS TAVERN

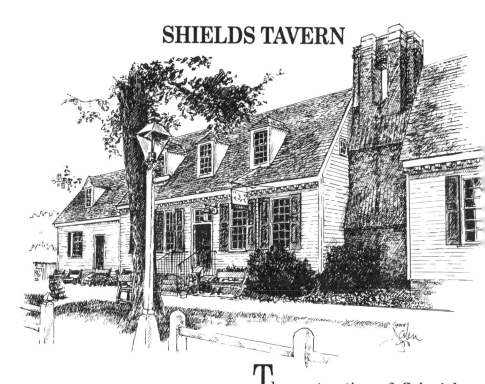

The restoration of Colonial Williamsburg, in revealing facts about early Virginians, has brought scholars together to develop new methods of "detecting" the past. Nowhere is the cooperation of researchers of different disciplines–archaeologists, architectural historians, and historians—more evident than in the recent interior reconstruction of Shields Tavern.

Rebuilt on original foundations in the early 1950s, the tavern's exterior approximated the building which stood there, in part, from 1708 until the early 19th century. The 1950s interior, used for staff housing, was never intended for exhibition.

When need for another operating tavern arose, a dig on the site turned up artifacts used in the tavern; pre-1700s domestic buildings in the Chesapeake area were examined for structural details; and tax records, wills, and inventories were studied for information about the furnishings and households of tavern keepers.

The tavern's interior was reconstructed to reflect the period of James Shields' occupancy, 1745 to 1750, and appropriate furnishings, staff dress, and menu were carefully determined.

Prepared in modern underground kitchens and served by costumed staff trained to answer your questions, foods served in Shields Tavern's 11 dining rooms are made of ingredients familiar to early guests. Many are adaptations of 18th century Virginia "receipts"—spit-roasted chicken and beef, Chesapeake Bay broiled seafood, chicken fricassée, meat pasties, and Indian corn pudding.

Shields Tavern is a reconstruction, but it is in a 175-acre National Register District, part of the restoration project that initiated interest in preservation in this country. At Shields Tavern you will not only learn about the past, but about REDISCOVERING the past—and you'll enjoy a delightful meal while you do so.

Shields Tavern, Duke of Gloucester Street, Colonial Williamsburg, is open for three meals a day, 7 days a week. (804)229-2141 or (800)HISTORY. All legal beverages are served, including Sunday, dress is casual (no tank tops or bare feet), and reservations are accepted. Winter hours may vary. AE, MC, V, personal checks. ($$$)

SHIELDS TAVERN
WILLIAMSBURG HOLIDAY PIE

One 10-inch unbaked
  deep pie shell
2 medium
  Granny Smith apples,
  peeled, cored, and sliced
1 Tablespoon flour
2 Tablespoons sugar

Pinch of cinnamon
6 ounces fresh cranberries
1/2 cup water
4 Tablespoons sugar
1 1/2 cups
  purchased mincemeat
Streusel topping*

In bowl, mix apples with next 3 ingredients and set aside. In saucepan, cook cranberries with water and sugar until berries just soften. Assemble pie: spread mincemeat on crust, apple mixture on top, then cranberry mixture. Spread Streusel on top and bake in 350 degree oven 35 to 40 minutes, or until golden brown.

*For Streusel Topping: Rub together 8 Tablespoons cold butter, 3/4 cup flour, and 4 Tablespoons sugar until mixture resembles small peas.

GADSBY'S TAVERN

$\mathbf{T}$obacco trade flourished in Virginia after Indian troubles ended, and a warehouse established on "Great Hunting Creek" in 1732 developed into an important port, named for an early Scottish settler. In 1749 a town was laid out by the county surveyor and his young assistant, George Washington.

A tavern stood on the southwest corner of Royal and Cameron before 1752; Washington traded with 3 different proprietors. Sold to John Wise in 1782, it was enlarged or rebuilt by 1785, achieving its present Georgian style. Its adjoining 3-story "City Hotel" was built in 1792.

John Gadsby, an Englishman, leased the tavern in 1796, when it had grown to ten buildings—stables, kitchens, and laundry—around a courtyard. It was described as "the best house of entertainment in America." Among frequent guests were many founders of this country and the first six Presidents of the United States.

Ballroom woodwork was removed to the Metropolitan Museum in 1929, and there was an outcry against further desecration of this architecturally and historically important building.

It was rescued by the American Legion in 1929, restored, and maintained by a number of history-minded organizations. The original doorway was returned in 1949.

Acquired by the city in 1972, the tavern was again restored, and reopened in 1976. Gadsby's Tavern is a National Historic Landmark in a 100-block National Historic Landmark District.

The earlier building houses the Gadsby's Tavern Museum, and the former City Hotel is again a tavern, with costumed staff entertaining and serving excellent American food with 18th century specialties, in a candlelight ambience you won't soon forget.

Popular Prime Rib is served with Yorkshire Pudding, Colonial Game Pye is a crust filled with vegetables and chicken or game in a cream sauce, and George Washington's Favorite Duck with Madeira Sauce might well become your favorite, too.

There's lighter fare at lunch—generous open-faced sandwiches, quiche, crab cakes, and chicken curry—and desserts include English Trifle, homemade fruit cobblers, several "pyes," and Scottish Apple Gingerbread with cinnamon icing.

Gadsby's Tavern, 138 North Royal Street, Alexandria, is open for lunch Monday through Saturday, 11:30 a.m. to 3 p.m., for dinner 7 days a week, 5:30 to 10 p.m., and for Sunday brunch 11 a.m. to 3 p.m. "Publick Table" on Sunday and Monday nights is a 3-course, fixed price, 18th-century meal with entertainment. (703)548-1288. All legal beverages are served, including Sunday, dress is casual, although most men wear coat and tie, and reservations are recommended. AE,CB,DC,MC,V. ($$)

GADSBY'S FUDGE PYE

One 10-inch
  unbaked pie crust
2 1/2 ounces flour
4 ounces cocoa

Dash of cinnamon
3 sticks margarine
4 eggs
1/4 cup chopped walnuts

Measure and mix dry ingredients. In bowl, cream margarine and eggs, add dry ingredients, mix in walnuts, and pour into crust. Bake at 350 degrees about 25 minutes, or until top breaks. Serve with whipped cream.

MR. PATRICK HENRY'S INN

Patrick Henry was thin, intense, a bit defensive, and had failed at farming and storekeeping before reading law; admitted to the bar at age 24, he became popular after a speech declaring that a ruler who breaks faith with his subjects loses the right to their loyalty.

Two years later, in 1765, he was elected to the Virginia legislature, where he protested the Stamp Act and wrote the "Virginia Resolutions," asserting the right of colonies to govern themselves. Defending this, he made his famous "... if this be treason, make the most of it" speech.

A radical among rebels, he served in both Continental Congresses, and at the Second Virginia Convention in St. John's Church in Richmond, his flaming oratory ended with, "... give me liberty or give me death!", resulting in the arming of the Virginia Militia—and war.

Just a block from the church, a prosperous middle-class suburb called "Church Hill" developed in the early 19th century. As the St. John's Church Historic District, it was placed on the National Register in 1970.

In Church Hill, about 1858, William Catlin built a house at

the northeast corner of Broad and 23rd streets. A Greek Revival-style, side-hall town house, it shows the skill of William Mitchell, a Black brick mason and father of Maggie Walker, first American woman bank president.

The corner house and its neighbor opened in 1976 as a restaurant and inn named for Patrick Henry. Jim and Lynn News, innkeepers, restored and furnished the two buildings, and established an eclectic menu that features fresh Chesapeake Bay seafood, herbs from the inn's garden, and homemade breads and desserts.

Backfin crab cakes are baked in puff pastry, Roast Duckling is glazed with honey and pink peppercorns, and grilled Medallions of veal are served with red pepper concassée and wild mushroom risotto.

Constantly changing desserts might be Crème Brûlée, Chocolate Orange Cheesecake, Chocolate Pâté on Raspberry Sauce, or fudge-like Chocolate Walnut Caramel Torte.

Mr. Patrick Henry's, 2300-02 East Broad Street, Richmond, is open Tuesday through Saturday for lunch, 11:30 a.m. to 2:30 p.m., and for dinner 5:30 to 10:30 p.m. Sunday brunch is 11:30 a.m. to 3 p.m. Light fare is served in the Pub, 5 p.m. to 12:00 midnight, Monday through Saturday. (804)644-1322. All legal beverages are served, most men wear coat and tie (patio and pub are informal), and reservations are recommended. There are 4 overnight suites. AE,DC,MC,V. ($$$)

MR. PATRICK HENRY'S
SOUTHERN STYLE PEANUT SOUP

6 cups seasoned
  chicken stock
3 to 3 1/2 cups
  creamy peanut butter
Pinch celery salt
White pepper and salt

1/2 cup heavy cream
Unsweetened
  whipped cream
Chopped honey-roasted
  peanuts

Strain stock through cheesecloth into large pan; bring to boil and whisk in peanut butter. Add seasonings to taste, reduce heat, and whisk in cream. Skim off foam and serve, garnished with whipped cream and peanuts. Serves 10.

THE FRENCH BETSY

On the site of a 1645 fort at the falls of the Appomattox River, Petersburg was laid out in 1748 and consolidated with three nearby settlements in 1784. It was a busy inland port of 3,000 by 1791, according to George Washington.

When it was incorporated in 1850, Petersburg rivaled Richmond with tobacco warehouses, flour and cotton mills, and iron foundries.

In the War Between the States, the city was spared until 1864, although it sent 17 companies to the front. Railroads converging in Petersburg made it Richmond's last defense, and Grant, after heavy losses, pursued Lee's army into battle and a 10-month siege. Casualties were enormous—42,000 Union and 28,000 Confederate soldiers—on the largest battlefield in the country.

Along the Appomattox waterfront, Petersburg's damage was heavy; one destroyed building had an unusual history. In 1810 there were 1089 free Blacks in Petersburg. A waterfront tavern owned by a free Black Frenchwoman, Betsy Allenque, passed to Peebles and White, wholesale grocers, and the name

"French Betsy" appeared on the deed.

That building was exploded to stop a serious fire in 1815; its replacement was lost to bombardment. The present structure, built in 1880, with the other two buildings in the Appomattox Ironworks complex, dating from 1790 and 1805, was placed on the National Register in 1976.

Opened by Ann Peckinpaugh as an antiques shop in 1975, the little building acquired a soda fountain in 1978, and gradually became a restaurant. The French Betsy provides a wide variety of food in an unusually interesting environment—evidence of the building's use as a pipe shop is visible in overhead cranes.

Hot and cold sandwiches, handmade burgers, and salads (great chicken salad) dominate lunch; candles and tablecloths change the mood for dinners of scampi, Chicken Amelia (boneless breast sautéed with wine and mushrooms), bacon-wrapped quail, and 10-ounce Delmonico steaks.

Ann's desserts are famous: fruit cobblers, Italian cream cake, six-inch chocolate chip cookies, and brownie-like Chocolate Chess Pie topped with whipped cream.

The French Betsy, 20 West Old Street, Petersburg, is open Tuesday through Thursday, 11 a.m. to 9 p.m.; Friday and Saturday 11 a.m. to 10 p.m.; and Sunday brunch 11 a.m. to 3 p.m. (804)732-1553. All legal beverages are served, including Sunday, dress is "comfortable," but dressier in evenings, and reservations are accepted. MC,V. ($$)

FRENCH BETSY HOMEMADE MINTS

8 ounces cream cheese
4 ounces butter
  or margarine
2 Tablespoons
  crème de menthe

1 pound powdered sugar
Additional
  powdered sugar

Place first 4 ingredients into food processor and blend. Sift additional sugar on tray; pour mixture into sugar, and work sugar into mixture. Place in rubber molds, form into fancy shapes, or roll into slender log and slice into small, bite-sized pieces. Store in covered container.

THE RED FOX INN

The town of Middleburg, half-way between Winchester and Alexandria, was laid out by Leven Powell in 1787 on a road that crossed his land. Facing that road, Noble Beveridge built two large structures on opposite corners of Madison Street. A brick house and store were built in 1825, and a similar stone building in 1827. Both have served as taverns, leading to understandable confusion.

Middleburg grew slowly, reaching a population of 391 by 1830, when Thomas Noland advertised the Mansion House, a superior tavern in Beveridge's stone building. After renovation in 1897, it was called "Beveridge Inn," and by 1900, "Middleburg Inn." Rented as apartments in the 1920s and '30s, it was extensively remodeled and opened as The Red Fox Tavern in 1941. Its most recent renovation was in 1976, when it became The Red Fox Inn under its present ownership.

At the center of the unofficial capital of the hunt country, Middleburg is a quaint village of mostly early 19th century buildings. The Middleburg Historic District was placed on the National Register in 1982.

As with any old building, legends abound about the Red

Fox. A recurring one is that it was surveyed by George Washington in 1731; Mr. Washington was born in 1732, and surveyed nearby lands—in 1774. Another possibly resulted from transposition of numbers on an early tavern sign: 1827 became 1728.

At any age, The Red Fox Inn is charming. Beneath smoke-darkened timbers or in Williamsburg-style dining rooms, you'll find baked chicken breast stuffed with boursin cheese, sautéed scallops in sherry and mushrooms, and tremendous porterhouse steaks. Lunch provides hearty sandwiches, "Middleburgers" and chicken in phyllo pastry. Soups are substantial, there's different pasta every day, and desserts such as Chocolate Chambord Torte, Three Nut Chocolate Torte, and Bread Pudding with Bourbon Sauce.

The Red Fox Inn, 2 East Washington (US 50), Middleburg, is open 7 days a week. Breakfast is 8 to 10:30 a.m., lunch is 11 a.m. to 3 p.m. (light fare 3 to 5 p.m.), and dinner 8:30 p.m. Sunday lunch/dinner is 12:00 noon to 3 p.m., dinner 3 to 8 p.m. (703)687-6301. All legal beverages are served, including Sunday, most men wear coat and tie (not required) and reservations are strongly suggested, especially on weekends. There are 23 overnight units in 4 historic buildings. AE,MC,V. ($$$)

RED FOX INN CRAB CAKES

3 eggs
3/4 to 1 cup mayonnaise
1/2 cup minced onions, drained
1/2 cup minced celery, drained
1 to 1 1/2 cup bread crumbs
1/4 cup lemon juice
2 Tablespoons Old Bay seasoning
3 Tablespoons Worcestershire sauce
1 teaspoon black pepper
2 pounds fresh lump crab meat
Oil for frying

In large bowl, mix first nine ingredients well; add crab meat and toss lightly. Form into patties and broil or fry in shallow oil. Serves 8.

BATTLETOWN INN

The beautiful Shenandoah Valley was the home of Tuscarora and Shawnee Indians; their road through the valley became a main route during westward expansion.

· In the 1730s, frontiersmen from Pennsylvania, reinforced by land-hungry immigrants, poured down the valley to settle beyond the Blue Ridge. National groups formed new communities, keeping together and accounting for ethnic-sounding place names.

Young George Washington began his surveying career in the employ of Lord Thomas Fairfax in 1748; presumably paid in land, he was soon a large landholder, requiring each tenant to plant four acres of apples, a crop still important to the area's economy.

Winchester was settled in 1743, after Frederick County was formed from Orange County. By 1755, when Lieutenant Colonel George Washington returned to build Fort Loudoun, Winchester had grown into a respectable town.

Not so the brawling little tavern community called "Battletown," nine miles away. It, too, was destined to be civilized, and in 1798, a town was laid out on property belonging to Benjamin Berry. Renamed for Berry, it grew rapidly, becoming county seat when Clarke County, named for George Rogers Clark (despite the misspelling of his name), was formed from Frederick County in 1836. By 1840 it had a fine Roman Revival Courthouse in a cluster of substantial buildings.

One of these was the two-story Federal-style brick structure that houses Battletown Inn. Chef Joseph and Nadja Byoral took charge in February, 1990, after the lease on their Charlottesville restaurant expired. Southern and Continental delicacies are prepared individually, from fresh ingredients, and served in welcoming, low-ceilinged rooms with wide board floors, and walnut tables scattered among antiques.

Special here are Yaegerschnitzel (breaded veal with cream and mushrooms), Smothered Chicken, baked Virginia ham, and roast leg of lamb with homemade mint jelly.

Several coffee-liqueur combinations make a nice dessert, or you might prefer an almond-scented caramel custard, chocolate mousse, or crêpes stuffed with scarlet lingonberries from Sweden.

Battletown Inn, 102 West Main Street, Berryville, may be reached from I-81 by exiting at VA 7. Drive east to Berryville cut-off. Inn is 1 block before the first traffic light, on the left. It is open Tuesday through Saturday for lunch, 11:30 a.m. to 2:30 p.m., for dinner, 5 to 10 p.m.; Sunday brunch is 11:30 a.m. to 3 p.m. (703)955-4100. All legal beverages are served, including Sunday, dress is casual, and reservations are recommended. The inn has 12 overnight rooms. AE,MC,V. ($$$)

BATTLETOWN SPOON BREAD

1 cup boiling water	1 1/2 teaspoons
1/2 cup corn meal	baking powder
1/2 cup milk	1 Tablespoon
1/2 teaspoon salt	softened butter
	2 eggs, well beaten

In bowl, pour boiling water over meal; mix in remaining ingredients, and pour into buttered casserole dish or individual ovenproof dishes. Bake at 400 degrees 20 to 25 minutes or until golden. Top with butter and serve at once.

THE OLD HARDWARE STORE RESTAURANT

Land speculators in the 18th century seldom lived on their lands, preferring to lease or hold them until they could sell at a profit. In the Blue Ridge foothills along the Rivanna River, land patents were first issued in 1727, and the people who did settle there in the next ten years, and their descendants, had a profound influence on the development of this country.

Among the first generation born in the area were Thomas Jefferson, Meriwether Lewis, and William and George Rogers Clark; without Jefferson, the United States might not exist, at least in its present form; without the combination of his intellect and daring and the bravery and perseverance of Lewis and the Clarks, our western border might well be east of the Mississippi River.

In 1762, around the new courthouse, a town was laid out and named for Queen Charlotte. The economy was supported by trade from surrounding farms, and the cultural life was enhanced by the University of Virginia Mr. Jefferson founded in 1819.

Charlottesville's downtown area still contains many 19th century buildings of various architectural styles. In 1976, part of Main Street was made into a downtown Pedestrian Mall. As part of the Charlottesville and Albemarle County Courthouse Historic District, it was placed on the National Register in 1982.

Anchoring the mall is an 1895 hardware store, converted into an interesting mixture of shops and restaurants. Part museum, part old-fashioned drugstore, beautifully restored and utilized, its walk-through eating area is a friendly "hometown restaurant," with good, imaginative food at popular prices.

The lengthy menu offers legendary sandwiches, quiches, crêpes, burgers, and variety salads, with a few dinners (curried chicken, barbecued ribs, Virginia ham steak) and a glass case of pastries you won't believe. Servings are huge, service is helpful, and you can still get a REAL milkshake at a real soda fountain.

The Old Hardware Store Restaurant, 316 East Main Street Mall, Charlottesville, is open Monday through Saturday. Coffee and pastries are available after 10 a.m.; the restaurant is open from 11 a.m. to 9 or 9:30 p.m. weeknights, to 10:30 or 11 p.m. Friday and Saturday. (804)977-1518. All legal beverages are served, dress is "polite," and reservations are accepted, especially for parties of 6 or more or for private rooms. DS,MC,V. ($$)

OLD HARDWARE STORE MALIBAR HILL CURRIED CHICKEN SALAD SANDWICH

5 cups chopped
  chicken white meat
2 Tablespoons lemon juice
1/2 cup heavy sour cream
1/2 cup mayonnaise
1 1/2 teaspoons
  curry powder

1 Tablespoon
  grated fresh onion
1/2 cup finely sliced celery
1 cup white seedless
  grapes
1/2 cup raisins
Salt and black pepper

Combine all ingredients; serve mounded on toasted English muffin halves.

THE JOSHUA WILTON HOUSE

Thomas Harrison and his wife Sara chose for their home in 1739 the intersection of the Indian road and the Spotswood trail, in a lovely part of the Shenandoah Valley. The stone house they built about 1750 still stands.

Harrison laid out fifty acres of his land for a town, and was instrumental in having it named seat of Rockingham County. The first courts were held in his home, and he gave land to the county for a courthouse in 1779.

Harrisonburg became the trading center for a considerable area, and although disrupted by several nearby skirmishes, it was not damaged by the War Between the States.

In 1865, Joshua Wilton migrated to Harrisonburg from Canada, and established himself rapidly as a merchant. Facing a generous lawn in a fashionable section of Main Street, the two-and-a-half story brick house he built in 1890 is remarkable for its profuse embellishments in Queen Anne, Gothic Revival, and Italianate styles.

The Joshua Wilton house was placed on the National Register in 1979, and was carefully restored for use as a restaurant and inn by Craig and Roberta Moore.

Chef Craig's "Regional cooking with Classical influences" has won enthusiastic fans; each dish, beautifully presented, is unique. Ingredients show concern—tuna is line caught, veal is free-range, and trout are locally raised—and their combination shows creativity.

Roasted quail are stuffed with veal sausage, grilled lamb chops are served with minted Zinfandel glaze and Norwegian Salmon,dusted in assorted peppercorns, is seared with smoked scallops.

Even salads are distinctive. For dessert, you might try a homemade sorbet (often strawberry, peach, or champagne), whipped cheesecake, Melissa's chocolate gâteau with ganache, or roasted-banana/white chocolate cream pie, topped with chocolate shavings.

The Joshua Wilton House, 412 South Main Street, Harrisonburg, is open for dinner Tuesday through Thursday, 5:30 to 9 p.m., Friday and Saturday to 10 p.m. Sunday brunch is 11:30 a.m. to 2:30 p.m.; Wednesday Afternoon Tea is 3 to 5 p.m. (703)434-4464. All legal beverages are served, including Sunday, "proper attire" is required, and reservations are suggested. There are 5 overnight rooms. AE,MC,V. ($$)

JOSHUA WILTON HOUSE
WHITE CHOCOLATE HAZELNUT CHEESECAKE

Prepared crust*
1/2 cup roasted hazelnuts
1/2 cup chopped
  white chocolate
24 ounces cream cheese
1 cup brown sugar

1 Tablespoon vanilla
3 Tablespoons
  coffee liqueur
2 eggs + 4 eggs
3 Tablespoons
  crème de cacao

Spread nuts and white chocolate over cooled crust and set aside. In large bowl, whip cream cheese and sugar until fluffy; blend in flavorings and 2 eggs, then add 4 eggs one at a time, mixing only until incorporated. Add crème de cacao and pour over crust. Bake in water bath at 350 degrees 40 minutes, or until set. Serves 10.
*For Crust: Combine 1 cup graham cracker crumbs, 1/2 cup melted butter, and 1/4 cup brown sugar. Line bottom of 10" springform pan, and bake 8 minutes at 350 degrees.

THE WILLSON—WALKER HOUSE

This pretty hillside village seems far removed from battlefields, but its history is tied to conflict, and two of America's ablest and most revered military leaders lived, and are buried, here.

Thomas J. "Stonewall" Jackson, a West Point graduate, taught at Virginia Military Institute for ten years, until 1861. His Confederate Valley Campaign is exemplary use of a small force, with speed and secrecy, to confound and defeat overwhelming numbers. The Confederacy never recovered from his accidental death in 1863.

Robert E. Lee, who served in the United States Army thirty-five years, was a graduate, later superintendent, of West Point. As beloved leader of Confederate forces, his masterful understanding of field defenses made the best use of an amateur army, outnumbered and underequipped. President of Washington College (Later Washington and Lee), after the War, his dignified acceptance of defeat helped reunite the country.

Their presence is still felt in Lexington.

William Willson, merchant, postmaster, and treasurer of Washington College, built a Classical Revival house on Main

Street hill in 1820. The massive, pedimented portico, altered when the steep street was drastically graded in 1851, changed again in 1911, when Harry Walker, a Black grocer, lowered the first floor to street level for his market.

As part of the Lexington Historic District, a National Historic Landmark, the Willson-Walker House was placed on the National Register in 1971.

Purchased from Walker's descendants in 1983 by Josephine Griswold, the house was returned to its earlier appearance—requiring eighteen months. In its graceful dining rooms, her "Eclectic New American Cuisine" produces crisp new tastes you won't find anywhere else.

Medallions of venison are sautéed with port and boysenberries; mountain trout are sauced with capers, sun-dried tomatoes, and lime; and pork tenderloin is combined with pecans and ginger.

Desserts include Chocolate Truffle Terrine with raspberry sauce, Warm Fruit Tart with orange hard sauce, and Maple Pecan-Praline Cream Pie.

The Willson-Walker House, 30 North Main Street, Lexington, is open Tuesday through Saturday. Lunch is 11:30 a.m. to 2 p.m. (no Saturday lunch December to April), dinner is 5:30 to 9 p.m. (703)463-3020. All legal beverages are served, dress is casual, and reservations are suggested, requested on Friday and Saturday. AE,MC,V. ($$)

WILLSON-WALKER HOUSE
RASPBERRY CORDIAL CREAM PIE

Crust*
2 cups whipping cream, divided
8 ounces large marshmallows

2/3 cup raspberry cordial
Whipped cream and grated chocolate for garnish

In heavy saucepan, place 1 cup cream and marshmallows; heat until melted. Add cordial, cool to "room temperature". Whip remaining cream firm; fold into mixture, fill crust, and freeze. Serves 8.
*For crust: In food processor, grind 5 ounces chocolate graham crackers with 1/4 cup pecans. Add 2 Tablespoons melted butter, press into 9" or 10" pie pan and chill. Bake at 375 degrees 5 minutes.

MARTHA WASHINGTON INN'S FIRST LADY'S TABLE

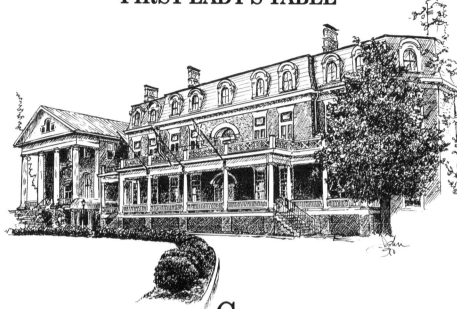

Colorful explorer and frontiersman Dr. Thomas Walker was granted land in southwestern Virginia in 1752. Black's Fort, established on a buffalo crossing, became the center of 120 acres donated for a county seat in 1778, after Washington County was formed from Fincastle County.

Later called "Abingdon," the town that developed around the fort is characterized by 19th century brick buildings in various architectural styles. The largest of these—one of the largest in Virginia—is a hilltop house erected in 1832 by Colonel Francis Preston for his large family.

Preston died in 1835, and in 1858, the house was sold to become Martha Washington College. Enlarged, it remained open during the War Between the States, despite financial troubles and one of General George Stoneman's raids that destroyed most of East Main Street.

The college closed in 1932. The buildings, used briefly to house actors at the experimental Barter Theatre, were leased in 1935 to become an inn.

As part of the Abingdon Historic District, Martha Washington Inn was placed on the National Register in 1970.

Purchased in 1984 by The United Company, the "Martha" underwent a $6 million renovation that made it one of the stellar hotels of the Southeast. Appropriately for the building's past, and perhaps accounting for the outstanding food and service, the inn's management is female.

In the elegant First Lady's Table, beneath the Greek Revival-style left wing, Continental food and some traditional Southern dishes are served. Boneless chicken breasts, sautéed with country ham and mushrooms, are topped with broccoli and Hollandaise; lamb chops are sauced with burgundy; and pork tenderloins are stuffed with mushrooms and corn bread.

Among desserts are flaming table-side preparations of Bananas Foster and Cherries Jubilee, and cheesecakes such as Chocolate-Peanut Butter and Orange-Grand Marnier.

Martha Washington Inn, 150 West Main Street, Abingdon, is open 7 days a week. At First Lady's Table, breakfast is 7 to 10 a.m. (buffet on Sunday), lunch is 11:30 a.m. to 2 p.m., and dinner is 5:30 to 10 p.m. Monday through Thursday, 5 to 10 p.m. Friday and Saturday, and 5 to 9 p.m. on Sunday. (703)628-3161. All legal beverages are served, except Sunday; dress is "relaxed," although most men wear a coat; and reservations are requested, almost required on holidays and for Friday night seafood buffet. There are presently 61 overnight rooms; additional rooms are planned. AE,DC,DS,MC,V. ($$$)

MARTHA'S SPOON BREAD

1 1/2 teaspoons sugar
1 teaspoon salt
1 cup cornmeal
4 Tablespoons butter
1 1/4 cups boiling water

3 eggs
1 Tablespoon
 baking powder
1 1/4 cups hot milk

In large bowl, place sugar, salt, and cornmeal. Stir in butter and boiling water and cool. Beat eggs with baking powder and add to mixture. Stir in hot milk and pour into buttered casserole. Place dish in a pan with hot water and bake 35 to 40 minutes or until set. Serve hot.

INDEX TO RESTAURANTS

INDEX TO RECIPES

Bittersweet Chocolate Terrine, The Victoria, 19
Butterfinger Pie, Scrooge's Restaurant, 127
Chocolate Roulage, Cobb Lane - The Corner Cupboard, 21
Devonshire Cream with Crimson Sauce, Pewter Rose Bistro, 143
Fresh Fruit with Grand Marnier Sauce, Fearrington House
   Restaurant and Country Inn, 139
Fudge Pye, Gadsby's Tavern, 197
Helen's Pecan Pie, The Dogwood Inn, 29
Homemade Mints, The French Betsy, 201
Jefferson Davis Pie, Boone Tavern, 79
Moravian Gingerbread, Old Salem Tavern, 141
Pecan Crispies, The Ninth Street House, 97
Raspberry Cordial Cream Pie, Willson-Walker House Restaurant,
   211
Spanish Caramel Flan, Columbia Restaurant, 47
Williamsburg Holiday Pie, Shields Tavern, 195
White Chocolate Hazelnut Cheesecake, Joshua Wilton House Inn
   and Restaurant, 209

EGG AND CHEESE DISHES
Canadian Cheddar Cheese Soup, Morris Street Tea Room, 167
Savory Cheesecake Packed in Peppercorns, Primerose House, 155

PASTA
Crawfish Capellini, Café Vermilionville, 105
Scallops on Linguine with Red Pepper and Caper Butter Sauce,
   Jamie's French Restaurant, 37

PORK, LAMB, AND VEAL
Grenadine de Veau Bentley, Hotel Bentley, 103
Rack of Lamb Dijonnaise, The Breakers, 51
Veal New Orleans, Chef Hans' Restaurant, 101

POULTRY
Basil Chicken Rotini, Mère Bulles, 187
Honey Bourbon Chicken, Trumps at the Georgian, 59
Malibar Hill Curried Chicken Salad Sandwich, The Old Hardware
   Store Restaurant, 207
Marinated Chicken Breast, Major Grumbles, 27
Mulberry Garden Casserole, Turn of the Century, 189
Roasted Mint and Green Chili Chicken, Claire's, 137
Turkey Piccata, The Vintage House Restaurant, 147

SALADS AND DRESSINGS
Creamy Tarragon Dressing, The Greenhouse, 25
Cucumber Mousse, Science Hill Inn, 89

Kentucky Bibb Lettuce with Hot Bacon Dressing, The Whistle Stop
  Restaurant, 93
Magnolia Heritage Salad à la Maureen, The Silver Platter
  Restaurant, 119
Malibar Hill Curried Chicken Salad, The Old Hardware Store
  Restaurant, 207
Strawberry Pretzel Salad, Shelley's Iron Gate, 17

SAUCES
Crimson Sauce, Pewter Rose Bistro, 143
Dijon-Honey Sauce, Café on the Square, 39
Dijon Sauce for seafood or chicken, Cap's Place Island Restaurant,
  53
Dilled Berry Relish for salmon, Gabrielle's at Richmond Hill Inn,
  149
Ginger Butter for seafood, Churchill's, 179
Grand Marnier Sauce for fresh fruit, Fearrington House Restaurant
  and Country Inn, 139
Green Chili Pesto, Claire's, 137
Honey Bourbon Sauce, Trumps at the Georgian, 59
Peanut Grilling Sauce for shrimp, Elizabeth on 37th, 73
Red Pepper and Caper Butter Sauce for scallops, Jamie's French
  Restaurant, 37
Rouille, Christian's, 109
Rum Sauce, Mary Mahoney's Old French House Restaurant, 129
Sorrel Sauce for salmon, The Pillars, 33
Wine Butter Sauce for poultry, The Vintage House Restaurant, 147

SEAFOODS AND FRESH WATER FISH
Baked Catfish, The Pompous Palate, 125
Barbecued Shrimp, Kolb's, 111
Bluefish Dijon, Cap's Place Island Restaurant, 53
Bouillabaisse, Christian's, 109
Ceviche, The Troutdale Dining Room, 173
Cioppino, Riverboat Landing Restaurant, 135
Coconut Shrimp with Dijon-Honey Sauce, Café on the Square, 39
Crab Cakes, Highlands: A Bar and Grill, 23
Crab Cakes, Red Fox Inn, 203
Crab in Phyllo Pastry, The Partridge Inn, 67
Crab Meat & Corn Bisque, Commander's Palace, 113
Crawfish Capellini, Café Vermilionville, 105
Eggplant and Crab Medallions, Vive la Différence, 107
Grilled Norwegian Salmon with Dilled Berry Relish, Gabrielle's at
  Richmond Hill Inn, 149
Grilled Shrimp and Cherry Tomatoes with Peanut Grilling Sauce,
  Elizabeth on 37th, 73

Low Country Shrimp over Hoppin' John Rice, 82 Queen, 157
Minorcan Clam Chowder, Scarlett O'Hara's, 41
Mussels Gino, Dee Felice Café, 81
Oyster Mushroom Terrine, 400 East Capitol, 117
Oysters Maurice, Café Society, 191
Red Snapper with Ginger Butter, Churchill's, 179
Salmon with Sorrel Sauce, The Pillars, 33
Scallops on Linguine with Red Pepper and Caper Butter Sauce,
    Jamie's French Restaurant, 37
Scallops Orange Ginger, Toby's Corner, 43
Shrimp and Crab Fritters, Train Station Restaurant, 91
Shrimp and Scallops Tarragon, Victorian Village Bistro, 69
St. John's Crab and Pecan Fritters, Jordan's Grove, 45

SOUPS
Bisque of Clam and Chicken, Grove Park Inn and Country Club,
    151
Blackeyed Pea Soup with Collard Greens, Belmont Inn, 163
Bouillabaisse, Christian's, 109
Canadian Cheddar Cheese Soup, Morris Street Tea Room, 167
Cioppino, Riverboat Landing Restaurant, 135
Crab Meat & Corn Bisque, Commander's Palace, 113
Cream of Shiitake Mushroom Soup, Seven Oaks Restaurant, 165
Crème de Brie, The Abbey, 65
Gin and Tomato Soup, The Planters, 63
Gratin Savoyard, The Soup Kitchen, 177
Loaded Potato Soup, Bartholomew's, 95
Minorcan Clam Chowder, Scarlett O'Hara's, 41
Pleasant Hill Popcorn Soup, The Shaker Village of Pleasant Hill, 87
Roasted Red Pepper Soup, Alexander Michael's, 145
Southern Style Peanut Soup, Mr. Patrick Henry's Inn, 199
White Gazpacho, The Corner House, 183

VEGETABLES
Broccoli Bonneau, Bonneau's, 159
Carrot or Asparagus Soufflé, Beaumont Inn, 85
Cucumber Mousse, Science Hill Inn, 89
Eggplant and Crab Medallions, Vive la Différence, 107
Hoppin' John Rice, 82 Queen, 157
Kentucky Bibb Lettuce with Hot Bacon Dressing, The Whistle Stop
    Restaurant, 93
Rice Casserole, The Mendenhall Hotel, 123
Southern Sweet Potato Pone, Old Southern Tea Room, 121

DINING IN THE HISTORIC SOUTH
Mail to:
McClanahan Publishing House, Inc.
P. O. Box 100
Kuttawa, Kentucky 42055

Please send me _____ copies of

DINING IN THE HISTORIC SOUTH	**@ $ 14.95 each**
DINING IN HISTORIC KENTUCKY	**@ $ 14.00 each**
DINING IN HISTORIC TENNESSEE	**@ $ 14.00 each**
DINING IN HISTORIC OHIO	**@ $ 14.00 each**
Postage and Handling	**@ $ 2.50 each**

Kentucky residents add 6% sales tax
Total

Make check payable to McClanahan Publishing House
Ship To:
Name_____

Address_____

City_____State_____Zip_____

— —

DINING IN THE HISTORIC SOUTH
Mail to:
McClanahan Publishing House, Inc.
P. O. Box 100
Kuttawa, Kentucky 42055

Please send me _____ copies of

DINING IN THE HISTORIC SOUTH	**@ $ 14.95 each**
DINING IN HISTORIC KENTUCKY	**@ $ 14.00 each**
DINING IN HISTORIC TENNESSEE	**@ $ 14.00 each**
DINING IN HISTORIC OHIO	**@ $ 14.00 each**
Postage and Handling	**@ $ 2.50 each**

Kentucky residents add 6% sales tax
Total

Make check payable to McClanahan Publishing House
Ship To:
Name_____

Address_____

City_____State_____Zip_____